Every Day's a Holiday Diabetic Cookbook

More Quick & Easy Recipes Everybody Will Love

By
Art Ginsburg
Mr. Food

Featuring ADA Spokesperson
Nicole Johnson
Miss America 1999

American Diabetes Association

Cure • Care • Commitment℠

ADA Director, Book Publishing, John Fedor; *Mr. Food Editor*, Caryl Ginsburg Fantel; *ADA Editor,* Abe Ogden; *Mr. Food Creative Director,* Howard Rosenthal; *Production Manager,* Peggy M. Rote; *Cover and Page Design,* Joe Peppi; *Composition,* Circle Graphics; *Food Styling,* Howard Rosenthal, Patty Rosenthal, and Diane Dolley; *Nutrient Analysis,* Nutritional Computing Consultants, Inc.; *Printer,* Port City Press

Printed in the United States
1 3 5 7 9 10 8 6 4 2

∞ The paper in this publication meets the requirements of the ANSI Standard Z39.48-1992 (permanence of paper).

ADA titles may be purchased for business or promotional use or for special sales. To purchase this book in large quantities, or for custom editions of this book with your logo, contact Lee Romano Sequeira, Special Sales & Promotions, at the address below, or at LRomano@diabetes.org or 703-299-2046.

American Diabetes Association
1701 North Beauregard Street
Alexandria, VA 22311

Library of Congress Cataloging-in-Publication Data

Ginsburg, Art.
    Mr. Food every day's a holiday diabetic cookbook : more quick & easy recipes everybody will love / by Art Ginsburg.
      p. cm.
    "Featuring ADA spokesperson Nicole Johnson, Miss America 1999."
    Includes index.
    ISBN 1-58040-138-4 (pbk. : alk. paper)
    1. Diabetes–Diet therapy–Recipes. 2. Holiday cookery. I. Title: Mister Food every day's a holiday diabetic cookbook. II. Title: Every day's a holiday diabetic cookbook. III. Title.

RC662 .G548 2002
641.5'6314–dc21

                    2002066716

Dedicated to all those
committed to finding a cure for diabetes—

With sincere thanks
for your efforts to enable
every person suffering with this disease
to look forward to a healthy and full life.

Contents

Foreword

Nicole Johnson
Miss America 1999

What a pleasure and a blessing it is to be working on another cookbook with my dear friend, Mr. Food. It is our continued goal to provide you with quick and easy recipes and tips to help you live a healthier and better life.

Diabetes is striking our society at an unprecedented rate. Aside from teaching people how to enjoy foods, Mr. Food and I are committed to doing all we can to reverse the trend that is claiming so many. This book is our second step in the fight against diabetes. However, we need your help to meet our goals. Diabetes can be deadly, but it doesn't have to be. If we manage the condition properly—including eating right—diabetes won't get the best of us. But we want to remind you that eating right doesn't have to equal boring food.

Haven't we all asked the questions, "What are people with diabetes to do about holidays?" or, "How can we, as people with diabetes, enjoy the classic, rich foods that are common to a celebration and not wreck our meal plan?" What about, "I am sick of eating chicken and veggies every day. What else is there for me to eat and still remain healthy?"

The answers are simple: Eat like you have never eaten before! Eat healthy, eat powerfully, eat in a festive way. Celebrate each day—don't fall prey to misconceptions about diabetes, food, diets, and restrictions.

These questions are what led to the creation of this book. I have asked these same questions on many occasions. Quite frankly, as a person with diabetes myself, I was sick and tired of the holidays and holiday food not being enjoyable. Thankfully, Mr. Food and his staff came to the rescue with ideas to help me incorporate some of my favorite "holiday" foods into my daily routine. After more than nine years with diabetes, I am thrilled to be enjoying festive occasions once again.

This book is about much more than recipes, though. Mr. Food and I want you to adopt a new life philosophy about eating healthy. "Learn as if you were to live forever, live as if you were to die tomorrow." We want you to realize that every day can be a holiday! We don't have to subscribe to the philosophies of old about diabetes or other special meal plans. This book will show you how to eat healthier and be happier in spite of your health challenge. Say goodbye to the same old dishes day in and day out. I challenge you to make every day a holiday with Mr. Food and me!

Nicole Johnson

Nicole Johnson
Miss America 1999, Author of *Living with Diabetes*

Preface

Art Ginsburg
Mr. Food

Within months of publishing my first cookbook for people with diabetes, I was getting tons of mail asking if and when I'd be putting out a second one! Since so many people expressed frustration over not knowing how to keep their eating on track during holidays and on special occasions, I decided to focus on that in my next book.

Another thing I noticed was how people with diabetes wanted to do something to make their everyday meals more special, too. After all, everybody gets into a rut from time to time. It's easy to get bored with our careers, exercise programs, and, especially, our meals. But by making even a slight change and getting out of our normal routine—whether it's setting the table differently or making a new recipe—we can breathe new life into an otherwise humdrum day.

So here it is—my gift to you. With this book on hand, not only will birthdays, graduation parties, Thanksgiving, and other holidays be "normal" and enjoyable for you again, but every day in between can be a reason to celebrate, too.

A bonus of writing this book has been once again having the opportunity to work with so many people who either have diabetes or who are working to find its cure ... especially Nicole Johnson.

Nicole amazes me with how she manages her hectic schedule, which seems to be busier now than when she was Miss America. She does so much and still keeps her diabetes under control. Her personal recipes, tips, and experiences, which appear throughout this book, will be an inspiration to everyone, with or without diabetes.

I know this book is filled with all sorts of great ways to jazz up mealtime, but the real stars are the recipes themselves. There are over 140 tasty and good-for-us selections to choose from, including appetizers, main courses, and, of course, lots of festive holiday desserts. Not only are they creative, but they're all easy to make!

My administrative staff jumped at the chance to taste-test the recipes for another book of American Diabetes Association-approved recipes. "I can't believe something this rich (or sweet, or creamy) fits a diabetic meal plan!" was heard again and again. These tastes are sure to satisfy, as long as you stick to appropriate portion sizes.

So, what are you waiting for? Select a few recipes—either for an upcoming holiday or just for any day—and get started, because every day's a holiday when everything looks and tastes this special. Hope this helps you enjoy countless new reasons to say … **"OOH IT'S SO GOOD!!®"**

Mr. Food

Acknowledgments

Though I've written more than 30 cookbooks, I still can't get over how many people it takes to ensure that every detail is attended to.

Of course, the first person I have to thank is Nicole Johnson. Until I met her a few years ago, my knowledge of diabetes was limited—and I sure hadn't considered writing a cookbook for people living with the disease. Since then, Nicole and I have made a number of TV appearances together, and have brainstormed on what else we can do to increase awareness of diabetes, while helping those suffering from this disease. All that has brought us here, to our second cookbook. Nicole, you are a shining example that even with diabetes, it is possible to lead an active, fulfilling life.

I really look up to all the hard-working people at the American Diabetes Association who continue their research to find a cure, as well as those involved in educating and making life easier for people with diabetes. Special thanks go to John Fedor, Director of Book Publishing, as well as our ADA editor Abe Ogden, Sherrye Landrum, Associate Director of Publications, Peggy Rote, Production Manager, and Lee Romano Sequeira, Director of Special Sales & Promotions.

If it wasn't for my creative and editorial teams, I'd be totally lost. Thanks to Howard Rosenthal and Caryl Ginsburg Fantel for your insight and your care in organizing our ideas and information. Thanks also to Joe Peppi for once again creating an inviting book design and page format, making all this information usable and practical for my readers.

I truly appreciate the contributions of Joe Peppi in coordinating the recipe testing, and of Patty Rosenthal, Diane Dolley, and Cheryl Gerber in testing these recipes over and over to make sure they'll work for you every time. A big "muchas gracias" to Dio Gomez for keeping our kitchen in tip-top order.

Many thanks to Lee Barnes, Helayne Rosenblum, and Jerilyn Grunbaum for your hours of researching, writing, and assisting with all the phases of this project. Thanks also must go to my assistant Marilyn Ruderman and to Alice Palombo for always keeping my office and me on schedule and running smoothly.

As always, I appreciate being able to depend on Steve Ginsburg, Tom Palombo, and Chet Rosenbaum to manage the administrative end of the Mr. Food enterprise.

John Swanston, even though we connected more via answering machines and e-mail, I appreciate all your assistance on Nicole's behalf.

To everyone who wrote to let me know how my first diabetic cookbook has changed your life, sent me your own recipes, or asked when I was coming out with another cookbook … this one's for you.

Last, but certainly not least, I thank my beautiful wife Ethel and the rest of my family for your limitless patience and support. As I wrote in my first book: Together we can do wonders!

Popular Holidays & Events[*]

January
New Year's Day (1)
Chinese New Year
   (based on the lunar calendar—sometime
   between 1/10 & 2/19)
Martin Luther King, Jr. birthday celebrated
   (third Monday)
Super Bowl Sunday (usually the last Sunday)

February
Groundhog Day (2)
Mardi Gras
   (Tuesday before Ash Wednesday)
Valentine's Day (14)
Presidents' Day (third Monday)

March
St. Patrick's Day (17)
Spring begins (20)
Easter
   (specific date based on the lunar calendar—sometime
   between 3/22 & 4/25)

April
April Fool's Day (1)
Passover
   (specific eight days based on the
   Hebrew calendar)
Daylight Saving Time begins (first Sunday)
Income Tax Pay Day (15)
Earth Day (22)
Arbor Day (26)

May
May Day (1)
College Graduations (throughout the month)
Cinco de Mayo (5)
Mother's Day (second Sunday)
Memorial Day (last Monday)

* Dates indicated are the legal observances.

June
Flag Day (14)
Father's Day (third Sunday)
High School Graduations (throughout the month)
Summer begins (21)

July
Independence Day (4)
Bastille Day (14)

August
Back to School
  (specific dates vary throughout the U.S.)

September
Labor Day (first Monday)
National Grandparents Day
  (Sunday following Labor Day)
Rosh Hashanah
  (Jewish New Year, based upon Hebrew calendar)
Yom Kippur
  (Jewish Day of Atonement, based upon
  Hebrew calendar)
Autumn begins (23)

October
Columbus Day (second Monday)
National Boss Day (16)
Daylight Saving Time ends (last Sunday)
Halloween (31)

November
General Election Day
  (Tuesday following the first Monday)
Veterans Day (11)
Thanksgiving
  (fourth Thursday)

December
Winter begins (21)
Hanukkah
  (Jewish Feast of Lights, based upon
  Hebrew calendar)
Christmas (25)
Kwanzaa
  (Harvest festival celebration observed by African
  American families—12/26 through 1/1)
New Year's Eve (31)

Introduction

Frequently Asked Questions

There is a lot of information available about diabetes and its management, but so much of it is written very technically, making it hard for people diagnosed with the disease to find simple answers to even basic questions.

Once diagnosed, and frequently as part of regular diabetes care, you should meet with your physician and an RD (Registered Dietitian) per his or her recommendation. Read on to find out why, and the answers to other important questions. And remember, for specifics, always consult your physician or Registered Dietitian.

1. **What can a Registered Dietitian do for me?**

   A Registered Dietitian will act as your personal nutritional guidance coun-selor to help you manage your particular meal plan and control your blood sugars. You should stay in touch with your RD to keep current on the lat-est nutritional recommendations.

2. **My friends all take extra vitamins during the holiday season to keep them from getting run-down. Should I do this, too?**

   It's hard for everybody to get through that busy period between Thanksgiving and New Year's without going overboard with our eating! As is the case with most people, someone with diabetes who eats a good variety of fruit, vegetables, and proteins each day really shouldn't need to supplement his or her diet with vitamins. Of course, check with your physician and/or RD before regularly adding *anything* to your diet.

3. **If I limited my diet to the same few "safe" foods, wouldn't my glucose control be easier?**

   Yes, but why deny yourself when you don't have to? I want you to eat like every day is a holiday—you can, you know. Everybody needs vari-ety, and tasty meals can be nutritious, too. You just have to get creative with your meal planning, and that's what I'm here for! Instead of feeling denied, you can feel excited about eating again! Go through the recipes in this book, and you'll see that healthy, festive eating doesn't have to be boring. And if there's a diabetes organization in your area, find out about sharing recipes with others in a support group. That's a great way to add even more interesting dishes to your meal plan.

4. **On special occasions, I'd really like to have a glass of wine or a cocktail. Is that okay?**

   For the most part, adults with diabetes are not sworn off alcohol, but remember: MODERATION IS KEY. The ADA guideline for one drink is a 5-ounce glass of wine, a 12-ounce light beer, or 1-1/2 ounces of 80-proof distilled spirits. The ADA guidelines generally allow for two drinks a day for men and one drink a day for women. Always make sure you know what is in your drink. Example: Those summertime favorites like piña coladas and other rum drinks, and drinks with fruit juice are very high in sugar, and may affect your blood sugar levels more than beer or wine. And when you do choose to have a drink, make sure to eat something along with it.

5. Can weight loss really help my diabetes maintenance?
Absolutely! It can help most of us. Not only does being close to your target weight improve blood pressure and blood fat levels, reducing the risk of heart disease, but it also lowers the chances of your body impeding the effects of insulin. Often a bonus of weight control is the ability to cut back on medications, if you have type 2 diabetes. Why not make attaining your ideal weight your personal goal?

6. Nicole, with your demanding schedule keeping you away from home a good part of the year, how do you manage to stay on track with your meal plan?
I have made a commitment to test my blood glucose level often to stay in control of my diabetes. Honestly, it's still a struggle for me, and many times I don't feel like doing it, but I know it is necessary for my life and my busy lifestyle. I have testing equipment in all my travel bags and in my car, which helps avoid logistical problems, and I wear an insulin pump, which helps tremendously. I also exercise anywhere I can, even in shopping malls or hotel stairwells! And since I eat in restaurants often, I have learned that I don't have to be restricted to printed menus—you can always request different combinations of foods prepared the way you want them in restaurants.

7. At Thanksgiving, my mom makes the best Pumpkin Pie. Are sweets like that a total no-no?
Not necessarily. On holidays and special occasions, there are always so many tempting foods around, but losing control is out of the question! I know it's hard to stay on track while it seems like people all around you are eating all the Thanksgiving pie, Halloween candy, and Christmas cookies they want. You can indulge a little, but what's my key word? MODERATION. That means practicing portion control. Get help from my Portion Pointers on pages 11–12.

Simply put, here's why: The calories you consume should be ones that help, instead of "empty" calories found in sweets, which not only fill you up—leaving no room for "good" foods—but raise your blood glucose level and make you gain weight. Instead of adding sugar to your foods, experiment with different types of fruit juices, seasonings, or even applesauce—again, in moderation. Small amounts of sugar might be okay, depending on your personal situation; however, artificial sweeteners might hold the key to satisfying your sweet tooth. Of course, even with those, portion control is still crucial. Take a look at pages 13–15.

So, as long as it's not totally against your meal plan, have a small slice of that holiday pie, or a smidgen of Valentine's Day chocolate. Just compensate for it by eating a little less bread, potatoes, or pasta, and taking a brisk walk around the block.

8. **Why does everybody make such a big deal about fat?**
The first thing to understand about fats is that they're *NOT* all the same, nor are they all bad! In fact, small amounts of fats are actually beneficial to us. For instance, the fat found in nuts like almonds, pistachios, peanuts, and cashews, and also avocados and olive and canola oils, is called monounsaturated. It is believed that this fat raises our HDL (good) choles-terol and lowers our LDL (bad) cholesterol levels. The next healthiest for us are the polyunsaturated fats. These are found mainly in vegetable oil, and they are also thought to raise HDL and lower LDL levels. You'll want to limit saturated (solid) fats, like those found in meat fat, lard, and, sorry, bacon. This type of fat often causes blood cholesterol to rise. According to the ADA, a healthy meal plan includes less than 30% of calories from fat with less than 10% of those derived from saturated fat.

9. **How can I cut the fat in my diet?**
Here are some tips that can be easily worked into your program. First, try to avoid fried foods. Go for lean meat and veggies that have been baked, broiled, or roasted. Stir-fry with lots of seasonings and a tiny amount of oil. Use canola oil or olive oil instead of lard. And here's the easiest of all: Choose low-fat or fat-free foods instead of regular foods. That's not so hard, huh?

10. **Nicole, what advice would you give to kids dealing with friends, fam-ily, and others who don't understand diabetes?**
Unless someone lives with this condition, they cannot fully understand its psychological, emotional, and physical effects. There will always be people who just can't grasp what diabetes is, so don't sweat it. One of the keys to overcoming your sense of isolation is to get plugged into a group with kids your age who have diabetes or face a similar challenge. Summer camps for kids with diabetes are an excellent way to meet others the same age who are facing the same issues as yourself. A good support system is key to diabetes care and control.

11. **Do I need to know about hypo- and hyperglycemia?**
Yes, it's very important to know what these are, and the difference between them, because the treatment is different. Hypoglycemia is when blood sugars fall too low. This can be caused by alcohol, too much insulin, or not eating enough. Symptoms can include sweating, turning pale, having trouble paying attention, and a tingling sensation around the mouth. If this happens, quickly drink something with sugar in it, like reg-ular soda or juice, or eat a piece of candy. Hyperglycemia is having too much glucose (sugar) in the blood. Not enough insulin, overeating, and stress can all contribute to an attack. Signs include tiredness, excessive thirst, frequent urination, upset stomach, and a fruity smell to the breath. Treat with extra insulin, or less food. More serious cases require immedi-ate medical attention.

Serving Tips

Family-style "sit-down" meals are still popular for small gatherings. They can be casual or formal. You can make up individual plates in the kitchen (the way most restaurants serve), but setting everything on the table in bowls or on platters is true "family-style" serving—and that enables your guests to serve themselves whatever (and as much or as little as) they want. Here are some helpful serving tips:

- Sit in the seat closest to the kitchen so as not to disturb your guests when getting up during the meal.

- If you don't have enough room at just your kitchen or dining room table, it's time to bring out your folding table. It can be quite a compliment to be seated at the "kids' table."

- Whether it's a special occasion warranting your fine china, or a casual event calling for disposable paper and plasticware, there should be a place setting for each guest. And be sure to have extras of everything on hand, just in case.

- Be sure to use table pads if you need them to protect your table from heat and moisture. After that, there are no rules about covering your table, but there are so many festive tablecloth and place mat options available today, it just makes sense! Cloth napkins sure make everyone feel special, but paper and plastic tableware now come in an endless variety of colors, styles, themes, and textures. Some paper napkins even feel like linen! So why not go with pink and red for Valentine's Day; bright colors or patterns for a tropical meal; red, white, and blue for July Fourth … you name it!

- When setting your table, consider your menu and what people will need to enjoy it. Be sure to set soup spoons if you're serving soup, salad forks if serving salad separately from dinner, etc. Utensils should be used from the outside in, so if soup is being served first, the soup spoon should be set on the outside. If serving salad as a separate course, usually before the main course, the salad fork should be on the outside of the dinner fork. Additional forks or spoons for dessert or coffee would go above the plate(s).

Planning a Perfect Buffet

The choice of whether or not to serve buffet-style is up to you, but it's usually the easiest way to serve a large group of people—even though it means presenting a larger variety of food than you'd generally have for a sit-down meal. The better you know your guests and their food likes, the easier it'll be to know what to serve, but even if you don't know them too well, you can still offer enough choices to please everyone without it getting too complicated.

- Make certain to plan a good "traffic pattern." This will allow everyone to get through your buffet line as quickly and smoothly as possible. For example, don't put a buffet table in the corner of your kitchen. Try to keep it in the dining room or on a long table somewhere out of the main flow of party traffic. It'll be easier for you to get in and out of the kitchen if you don't have to maneuver around extra people!

■ Place the plates at the beginning of the buffet table, where the guests will start serving themselves. Next should come a salad, followed by a main course, side dishes, bread, and, finally, dessert. If room doesn't allow for the dessert to be on the table along with the rest of the food, bring it out later during the party and serve it on a separate table or a countertop. Cold and hot beverages should be on a separate serving table or countertop, too, if possible. If not, have those at the end of the buffet table. And don't forget the silverware! I think the easiest way to put that out is to roll individual sets of utensils in napkins in advance and place them at the end of the buffet table so that people don't have to balance them all the way through the buffet line.

■ Have a few cold foods and a few hot foods. That way there's a variety for people to choose from—and having just a few dishes to warm helps when you have a limited amount of oven and stovetop space. Try not to put these out too soon before serving time, and refill frequently.

■ Serve foods that vary in flavor and texture. People like options. For example, offer two contrasting main dishes and a few side dishes.

■ Don't forget serving pieces! Every bowl or platter of food should have at least one serving piece—and be sure it's one that's appropriate, like a large spoon for meatballs, a slotted spoon for coleslaw, tongs for salad, a fork for cold cuts, etc.

Dressing for Dinner

There's an expression that says we "eat with our eyes." I happen to agree with that! No matter how good food tastes, it has to look good, too, or people won't want to eat it. Now, I'm not saying that we need to spend hours making fancy decorations, or buy expensive table centerpieces. It just makes a meal feel special when our food and our tables look colorful. Here are a few simple garnishing tips:

■ Accent salads or other cold foods with thinly sliced lemons, cucumbers, or rings of different-colored bell peppers. And to make them look even fancier, before cutting, stripe the skin of washed cucumbers with a vegetable peeler or a fruit zester, or score the skin with a fork. Then slice away.

■ Use cleaned parsley, scallions, or different types of lettuces or greens (heartier types like endive, leaf lettuce, kale, romaine, and Salad Savoy are the best) for garnishing platters and individual plates. For example, it's easy to place a bit of green around a serving bowl and then place potato or macaroni salad in the bowl. Finish your garnishing by topping with a few cherry tomatoes, sliced hard-boiled eggs, or black or green olives.… Wow!

■ Decorate with strawberries or radishes by cutting thin slices three-quarters of the way through each and fanning them out. After cutting radishes this way, it's best to store them in icy cold water for about an hour so they really get a chance to "blossom."

- Great all-around toppers are fresh chopped parsley, scallion rings, and paprika. A sprinkle of any of them goes a long way.

- Fruit sure adds pizzazz! You can clean and cut almost any fruit into wedges or slices for adding quick color. Or get out your melon baller and garnish with melon balls. And you'll have a sure hit if you toss together 2 or 3 types of melon balls—maybe honeydew, cantaloupe, and watermelon—for serving in a watermelon basket. It's not hard to do, but if you'd rather keep it really simple, then maybe just cut a watermelon in half, scoop out and cut up the insides, then place the fruit back in the scooped-out watermelon "bowl" for serving.

- That same melon baller can be used for making scoops of butter to serve on pancakes or fish, or even piled on a serving plate to go along with your favorite bread or rolls. Butter balls can be made in advance, laid out on a cookie sheet, covered with plastic wrap, and kept frozen until ready to use.

- Besides dressing up our food platters, we can fancy up our tables, too. You can buy an arrangement of flowers for a table centerpiece, but a bunch of flowers loose in a vase are pretty, too (and usually less expensive). Fresh flowers are readily available at most supermarkets these days. They sure add a fresh look and scent to a buffet or dinner table (but be sure they're not so tall that people can't see one another across a sit-down dinner table).

- If you're really in the mood, make your own novelty decorations for placing around the house—and you can do this by using things that you've already got on hand. Drape a serape (a Mexican shawl) over a chair near your buffet table or put a piñata in the center of your Mexican buffet. Pumpkins, gourds, and baskets of apples sure say "Happy Harvest Time" on an autumn buffet. How 'bout putting party hats and streamers around the back of your New Year's or birthday buffet—or serve a Chinese dinner right from a wok and decorate with Chinese fans. Just talking about this puts me in the mood to celebrate!

- Don't forget the candles! They can create almost any mood—classy, romantic, or festive. Just be sure to put something under them to catch drips, and place them safely out of the reach of little and big guests (and pets, too), and away from curtains, furniture, and other flammables.

Now go ahead and have fun celebrating holidays and "regular" days. I bet your family and guests will be surprised by whatever you do to make them feel special—and so will you!

Understanding Food Terms and Package Labels

One of the best ways we can help ourselves control diabetes through our diet is by reading and understanding the labels on food packages. To help us make healthier choices, the Federal Department of Agriculture has established specific guidelines for labeling food products. This chart should make understanding food labels as simple as 1-2-3:

Package Wording	The Product Contains
Sugar-free	Less than 0.5 gram sugar per serving
No added sugar, Without added sugar, No sugar added	No sugars added during processing. This is *not* the same as "sugar-free." Consult the nutrition information panel for the total amount of natural sugar in this product.
Reduced sugar	At least 25% less sugar per serving than the traditional version of the food
Reduced-fat, Less fat	At least 25% less fat per serving than the traditional version of the food
Low-fat	3 grams or less of fat per serving
Saturated fat-free	Less than 0.5 gram saturated fat per serving
Fat-free	Less than 0.5 gram fat per serving
Light	50% less fat *OR* 1/3 fewer calories per serving than the traditional version of the food
Reduced sodium, Reduced salt	25% less sodium per serving than the traditional version of the food
Reduced cholesterol	At least 25% less cholesterol and 2 grams or less of saturated fat per serving than the traditional version of the food
Cholesterol-free	Less than 2 milligrams cholesterol and 2 grams or less of saturated fat per serving
Reduced calorie, Fewer calories	At least 25% fewer calories per serving than the traditional version of the product
Low-calorie	40 calories or fewer per serving
Calorie-free	Fewer than 5 calories per serving
Lean	Less than 10 grams fat, 4.5 grams or less saturated fat, and less than 95 milligrams cholesterol per serving and per 100 grams
Extra lean	Less than 5 grams fat, less than 2 grams saturated fat, and less than 95 milligrams cholesterol per serving

Once you get past the name of a product and its claims of being lighter in one or more ingredients, there's more to examine. Food packaging may contain health claims that explain the value of the product. For example, a food high in fiber and low in saturated fat could be claimed to reduce cholesterol levels and, therefore, a person's risk of heart disease if he or she consumes that product. I can't stress enough that you should read food labels completely and carefully and, if you have any questions about particular foods, ask your physician or Registered Dietitian.

In addition to meeting requirements for the definitions of claims made on food labels, the FDA also requires that virtually all food labels contain a nutrition label, called Nutrition Facts.

You shouldn't have to look too hard for this information, either, because the government regulates the size of the labels. It also has strict guidelines regarding the information that is contained in these labels. This means that we can count on their being large and clear enough to read and understand easily.

Here's a sample nutritional fact label and an explanation of what those numbers mean to us:

Nutrition Facts

1 — Serving Size 1 cup (228g)
2 — Servings Per Container 2

Amount Per Serving

Calories 260   Calories from Fat 120

	% Daily Value*
Total Fat 13g	**20%**
Saturated Fat 5g	**25%**
Cholesterol 30mg	**10%**
Sodium 660mg	**28%**
Total Carbohydrate 31g	**10%**
Dietary Fiber 0g	**0%**
Sugars 5g	
Protein 5g	

Vitamin A 4%	•	Vitamin C 2%
Calcium 15%	•	Iron 4%

* Percent Daily Values are based on a 2,000 calorie diet. Your daily values may be higher or lower depending on your calorie needs:

	Calories:	2,000	2,500
Total Fat	Less than	65g	80g
Sat Fat	Less than	20g	25g
Cholesterol	Less than	300mg	300mg
Sodium	Less than	2,400mg	2,400mg
Total Carbohydrate		300g	375g
Dietary Fiber		25g	30g

Calories per gram:
Fat 9 • Carbohydrate 4 • Protein 4

Source: Federal Department of Agriculture

1 Serving Size—This is what is considered standard for the item. You may find that your serving size fluctuates quite a bit depending upon how small or large a serving you and your family eat of a particular item. Please be realistic here and remember that portion control is a big factor in diabetes management.

2 Servings per Container—Again, the servings are just a guideline of what is considered average. This number should be adjusted depending upon your personal dietary needs.

3 To most of us, the important information is the amount of fat, cholesterol, sodium, carbohydrates, and nutrients contained in any food. That's why these are listed not only in grams or milligrams, but also as a percentage of an average person's daily allotment, based on a daily 2,000-calorie (or sometimes also a 2,500-calorie) diet.

Your own daily values for these items may be higher or lower, depending on your level of activity and your personal needs. Please note that since carbohydrates are found in sugar and starch, this is the main cause of increased blood glucose levels. The ADA recommends that carbohydrates make up no more than 55–60% of the total daily calories.

4 Only two vitamins, A and C, and two minerals, calcium and iron, are required to be listed on food labels. Food companies may voluntarily list others and, if they do, be sure to make that information work for you!

Some labels also list the approximate number of calories in a gram of fat, carbohydrate, and protein. When available, these numbers can be helpful in creating your meal plans.

Since the format of and information contained on food labels is supposed to be consistent from product to product and brand to brand, you can do your own comparisons and balance your food choices. Few foods provide 100% of a single nutrient, so the percentage values on the packages can help us make knowledgeable nutrition choices. As always, if you'd like further information on how to shape your own meal plan, the best place to start is with your physician and/or Registered Dietitian.

Portion Pointers

What do a tennis ball, a light bulb, and a computer mouse have in common? Keep reading and you'll find out.

Is it really such a big deal if you eat a smidgen more than what your meal plan calls for? You might think that an extra ounce of something here or there won't really affect anything, but put down that fork, because it *does* make a difference. Those extra calories add up, bringing you extra weight, making it that much harder to control diabetes. That's where portion control comes in.

I certainly don't expect anyone to run around with a food scale, so here are two easy ways you can measure your foods:

■ Try this with fruits and veggies: In the supermarket produce section, pick up small, medium, and large pieces of fruit in your hands and guesstimate their weight; then weigh them on the store's scale. How close are you? After doing this a few times, you'll be able to fairly accurately guess the weight of most fruit and veggies. That's the start of portion control!

■ Say you want to know what one cup of low-fat milk looks like. Will you always have to use a measuring cup? No way! Simply measure one cup of any liquid in a measuring cup, then pour the liquid into one of your regular drinking glasses. Mark or memorize where the liquid comes up to. It's so easy! This method can actually be applied to just about anything, from how much cereal to put in your bowl to how much oil you use to coat your skillet. It's always best to be aware of exactly what you're taking in.

When you eat out, portion control can get a bit tricky. If you go to a restaurant that serves large portions, then split your meal with your partner, or, better yet, right when your meal arrives, set aside half to bring home for lunch or dinner the next day.

Now for the tennis ball, light bulb, and computer mouse part. It's a table that references everyday objects to help you compare food portions:

2 tablespoons salad dressing	=	ice cube
3 ounces meat	=	deck of cards
Medium apple	=	tennis ball
Medium potato	=	computer mouse

Medium onion	=	baseball
1 cup cut fruit	=	average orange
1 ounce meat	=	matchbox
1/2 cup cooked pasta	=	ice cream scoop
1 ounce bread	=	CD case
1 cup broccoli	=	light bulb
2 tablespoons peanut butter	=	golf ball
1 ounce cheese	=	domino

After practicing these tips, you'll be able to tell the sizes of your portions just by looking at them. It's really not that hard, and, speaking of cards, balls, and dominoes, you can even turn it into a game! The winner? You, of course!

Substitution Savvy

Okay, so you have to make a few adjustments in your eating habits. Does that mean you'll have to give up tasty foods? No way! Making the switch from the traditional versions of your favorite foods to their lower-fat counterparts can be a snap, and I bet you're already using some lower-calorie foods. Keep going with that, and use this sensible guide to help you use healthier foods without losing the flavor you long for.

Instead of:	*Try this:*
Full-fat cheese	Low- or reduced-fat cheese, or a strong-flavored cheese (with those you can usually use half the amount a recipe calls for)
Regular fried corn or potato chips	Baked tortilla or potato chips, or pretzels
Heavy cream	Evaporated skim milk
Croissants	Bagels, pita bread
Whole eggs	Egg substitute, egg whites
Ground beef	Lean ground beef, ground turkey breast
Ice cream	Sherbet, frozen yogurt, low-fat ice cream
Sour cream	Fat-free sour cream or plain yogurt
Whole milk	Fat-free or 1% milk

Substituting lower-fat and lower-calorie foods is only one step in healthier eating, but there are several ways we can prepare or cook our meals that will make them better for us. Here are a few ideas:

- Instead of frying or sautéing, give baking, steaming, poaching, broiling, or grilling a try. These methods really cut down on fat.

- Use nonstick pots and pans because they require less fat to keep food from sticking.

- Use a splash of citrus juice—lemon, lime, or orange—in place of dressings to give foods zing without adding calories.

- With strong-flavored cheeses like blue, Parmesan, and Romano, simply cut down on the amount used; a little of those goes a long way!

- If you are limiting dietary cholesterol, eggs can still be a part of your meal plan, but in moderation. Two egg whites equal one whole egg, and there are also great egg substitutes in the egg section of your grocery store. Give those a try.

- When eating at home or eating out, watch what you drink! Drink water, unsweetened brewed iced tea, or unsweetened sparkling water instead of soft drinks, sugar-laden fruit juices, or milk shakes. A slice of fresh lemon or lime will add a zip to your water or iced tea, too.

- In restaurants, choose steamed vegetables instead of fat-laden side dishes, and ask for dressings, sauces, and condiments (low-fat and low-calorie, when possible) on the side so you can control your intake.

I know you're not going to make all these changes overnight, but given some time and a little practice, you'll have no problems putting together great-tasting, good-for-you meals. Trust me!

Sugar and Artificial Sweeteners

One of the first thoughts that goes through a person's head after being diagnosed with diabetes is, "Oh, no! I can never have anything sweet again!" Well, that was how it was years ago, when doctors believed that regular table sugar (sucrose) made blood glucose levels fly through the roof.

Hence, the arrival of artificial sweeteners. Along with their commercial availability came questions and concerns, such as "Can I bake with them?" and "Are they better for me than sugar?" I like to call these sweeteners "freebies" because they sweeten our foods without adding calories and raising blood glucose levels.

Before I tell you more about artificial sweeteners, you should know that, thanks to extensive testing, **the American Diabetes Association changed its nutritional recommendations in 1994 and reported that sugar doesn't affect blood glucose much differently than any other carbohydrate.**

Now don't go running out for a jumbo candy bar just yet. The ADA report stated that sugar could indeed be worked into diabetic meal plans set up by dietitians, with the understanding that sugar is not a "free food." Sugar counts as a carbohydrate and must therefore be substituted for other foods containing carbohydrates. And since sugar calories are "empty" calories, it's certainly preferable to choose carbohydrates that provide more nutritive value. *That's* why we can have sugar—in moderation.

Since many people with diabetes still use quite a lot of artificial sweeteners, let's take a look at four that are currently ADA- and Food and Drug Administration-approved:

1. Although there has been debate over its use since the early 1900s, **saccharin** is the most commonly used artificial sweetener in the United States. With a taste 300 times sweeter than sugar, saccharin, found in Sweet 'N Low®, works well in both hot and cold dishes.

2. **Aspartame**, a.k.a. NutraSweet® and Equal®, was discovered in 1965. Mild reactions, such as headaches and dizziness, have been reported from the use of aspartame, and people with PKU (phenylketonuria, a rare genetic disease) must avoid anything containing it. Aspartame tends to lose its sweetness when heated for long periods, so, when possible, it should be added to baked items toward the end of cooking, or sprinkled on after their removal from the heat.

3. Acesulfame-K, also known as **acesulfame potassium**, is sold under the brand name Sweet One®. Discovered in 1967, this sweetener is 200 times sweeter than sugar. Sweet One contains 1 gram of carbohydrate. Acesulfame-K can be used in baking, but produces finished items with a noticeably different texture than those made with sugar.

4. **Sucralose** is 600 times sweeter than sugar. This sweetener, known by the brand name Splenda®, is made from sugar and contains carbohydrates. People have been very successful cooking and baking with it, and it can also be added directly to foods.

Here's a helpful chart that converts sugar measurements to numbers of packets of no-calorie sweeteners. Many of the recipes in this book work well with either sugar or artificial sweetener. However, please note that since sugar is important to the volume and texture of most baked goods, you may find that you can replace just half the amount of sugar called for in a baked goods recipe with an appropriate sugar substitute. Experiment and see for yourself. **Don't forget: Moderate use of sugar is approved by the ADA in the majority of diabetic meal plans; use what works for your particular plan.**

Sugar Amount:		Equivalency in sweetener packets:
2 teaspoons	=	1 packet
1 tablespoon	=	1-1/2 packets
1/4 cup	=	6 packets
1/3 cup	=	8 packets
1/2 cup	=	12 packets
3/4 cup	=	18 packets
1 cup	=	24 packets
1 pound	=	57 packets

Remember that everyone reacts differently to various sweeteners, so discuss their use with your physician and dietitian, and use what works for you. And whether you choose to use sugar or artificial sweeteners—or a combination—test your blood glucose levels after you eat all sweet foods in order to determine their effect on you. Also ask your physician about increasing your insulin intake at those times when you know you will be eating sweet foods. Our goal with eating sweet foods should be to make sure they're physician- or dietitian-approved and as nutritious as possible.

Sodium Smarts

Did you know that our bodies require only about 220 mg of sodium (salt) per day, yet the average American takes in almost 5,000 mg per day? Wow! We really like our salt, huh? The American Diabetes Association recommends that people with diabetes (and actually everyone) keep their daily sodium intake to less than 3,000 mg, and those with mild or moderate hypertension stay under 2,400 mg per day.

We shouldn't cut sodium out of our diets completely, as our bodies need it to function properly. And what's my favorite word? MODERATION! Too little of most things is no good, and too much isn't good, either. Too much sodium can raise blood pressure, which in turn can raise the chances of developing heart disease or stroke.

So, you want to know how you're supposed to season your food without adding measurable amounts of sodium, right? That's easy! With a clove or two of chopped or pressed garlic, some onion, and, of course, fresh herbs. It can be so much fun to experiment with them, especially since fresh herbs are almost always available in the supermarket produce section.

Here's a simple seasoning trick that I've been using lately: using canned reduced-fat, low-sodium chicken broth in place of water when making rice or pasta—or just about anything that needs a little liquid. Keep a few cans on hand to help flavor almost anything you cook!

General Recipe Notes

If a recipe included here calls for "Salt to taste," then that recipe's nutritional analysis does not include salt as a separate ingredient, and you should be aware that the recipe's sodium level will increase if it is added.

Unless otherwise specified, onions and other produce items called for should be medium or "average"-sized.

Packaged food sizes may vary by brand. Generally, the sizes indicated in these recipes are average sizes. If you can't find the exact package size listed in the ingredients, whatever package is closest in size will usually work in the recipe, but please remember that using different products may alter the recipe's nutritional analysis. Experiment with different brands until you're satisfied.

As I mention throughout this book, always use the lightest ingredients possible. And just because a product's name includes the word "light," doesn't necessarily make it so. You need to read and know what you're looking for on package labels. (See "Understanding Food Terms and Package Labels" on page 8.) It's the best way to truly start lightening up your diet.

Appetizers

Fiesta Quesadillas

Serving Size: 3 wedges, Total Servings: 16

3 cups (12 ounces) shredded Mexican cheese blend

Eight 10-inch flour tortillas

1/2 cup bottled sliced jalapeño peppers, drained (optional)

1 Sprinkle 3/4 cup cheese over each of four tortillas; sprinkle jalapeño peppers evenly over the cheese. Top with the remaining tortillas, making sandwiches.

2 Lightly coat a large skillet with nonstick cooking spray. Heat over medium heat and place one tortilla sandwich in the skillet. Cook for 1 to 2 minutes per side, or until the cheese is melted. Remove to a covered platter and cook the remaining sandwiches one at a time.

3 Slice each finished quesadilla into 12 wedges and serve.

"Don't wait for a holiday to try these zippy south-of-the-border-turned-American favorites. Paired with bowls of traditional go-alongs, they're perfect as an appetizer, or even for a fast weeknight dinner. And if you want to hearty them up, just add some thinly sliced cooked chicken. Either way ... 'Ay qué bueno!!'—that's Spanish for 'OOH IT'S SO GOOD!!'"

Exchanges
1-1/2 Starch
1 High-Fat Meat

Calories............................199
   Calories from Fat............84
Total Fat.............................9 g
   Saturated Fat.....................5 g
Cholesterol........................19 mg
Sodium..............................321 mg
Carbohydrate....................20 g
   Dietary Fiber.....................1 g
   Sugars................................1 g
Protein...............................8 g

Raspberry Brie

Serving Size: 1/8 wedge, Total Servings: 8

1 round Brie cheese
(8 ounces)

1/4 cup raspberry preserves

1 tablespoon sliced almonds,
toasted

1 Place the Brie in a microwave-safe 9-inch pie plate.

2 Spread the raspberry preserves over the top and microwave at 50% power for 2 minutes, or until warmed through (see Finishing Touch).

3 Remove from the microwave and sprinkle with the almonds. Serve warm.

Exchanges
1/2 Carbohydrate
1 High-Fat Meat

Calories............................115
   Calories from Fat............73
Total Fat..............................8 g
   Saturated Fat......................5 g
Cholesterol........................25 mg
Sodium............................212 mg
Carbohydrate....................8 g
   Dietary Fiber....................0 g
   Sugars..............................5 g
Protein..............................4 g

Finishing Touch

Your guests' eyes will light up brighter than a Christmas tree when you serve this elegant "easy" surrounded by crackers, sliced French bread, and fresh seasonal fruit. If you prefer to heat this in the oven, you can bake the Brie at 350°F. for 15 to 20 minutes, or until heated through.

Cheesy Pecan Grapes

Serving Size: 3 grapes, Total Servings: 12

1 package (8 ounces) reduced-fat cream cheese, softened

1 package (4 ounces) crumbled blue cheese

36 seedless green grapes, washed & patted dry

1-1/2 cups chopped pecans

1 In a small bowl, combine the cream cheese and blue cheese; mix well. Add the grapes and mix gently to coat.

2 Place the chopped pecans in a shallow dish and roll the cheese-coated grapes in the pecans until completely coated.

3 Place the grapes on a platter. Cover, and chill for at least 2 hours before serving.

"No more boring party hors d'oeuvres! Celebrate holidays by pairing your favorite bubbly with these irresistible bite-sized surprises. Hey, why save these just for holidays?"

Exchanges
1/2 Carbohydrate
1 High-Fat Meat
1-1/2 Fat

Calories	188
Calories from Fat	147
Total Fat	16 g
Saturated Fat	4 g
Cholesterol	20 mg
Sodium	212 mg
Carbohydrate	7 g
Dietary Fiber	2 g
Sugars	3 g
Protein	5 g

Salmon-Stuffed Eggs

Serving Size: 2 egg halves, Total Servings: 12

1 dozen hard-boiled eggs, shelled

1 can (6 ounces) salmon, drained and flaked

1/2 cup light mayonnaise

1 tablespoon finely chopped fresh dill weed

1/8 teaspoon black pepper

1 Cut the eggs in half lengthwise and remove the yolks to a medium bowl; set aside the egg whites. Add the salmon, mayonnaise, dill, and pepper to the yolks; mix until well combined.

2 Spoon or pipe the mixture back into the egg whites (see below). Serve, or cover and chill until ready to serve.

Exchanges
1 Medium-Fat Meat
1 Fat

Calories	128
Calories from Fat	83
Total Fat	9 g
Saturated Fat	3 g
Cholesterol	224 mg
Sodium	222 mg
Carbohydrate	1 g
Dietary Fiber	0 g
Sugars	1 g
Protein	9 g

Did You Know...

there's a simple way to pipe this salmon mixture into the egg whites? Just place it in a resealable plastic bag and snip off a corner of the bag. Then you can pipe directly into the egg whites. Top each with a sprinkle of paprika and a sprig of fresh dill weed and, in no time, you've got a meal-starter that looks like it was made by a professional!

Marinated Mushrooms

Serving Size: 1/4 cup, Total Servings: 10

1 pound white mushrooms, washed and halved

1 medium onion, cut in half and thinly sliced

1/4 cup white vinegar

1/4 cup vegetable oil

2 tablespoons sugar

1/2 teaspoon dried oregano

1/2 teaspoon salt

1/4 teaspoon black pepper

1 Place the mushrooms in a medium saucepan and cover with water. Bring to a boil over high heat, then reduce the heat to medium-low and simmer for 20 minutes; drain and let cool.

2 In a glass container with a tight-fitting lid, combine the remaining ingredients; mix well. Add the cooked mushrooms, stir, cover, and chill for at least 2 hours before serving. Mushrooms can be stored in a tightly closed glass container in the refrigerator for up to 1 week.

"Mushrooms are a real favorite of mine! July 4th, Thanksgiving, or whenever, these are easy to fix for any holiday gathering. And the best part? For those of you having a hard time meeting the recommendations for veggies, this is an easy and tasty dish to incorporate into your meal plan."

Exchanges
1 Vegetable
1 Fat

Calories	77
Calories from Fat	53
Total Fat	6 g
Saturated Fat	0 g
Cholesterol	0 mg
Sodium	119 mg
Carbohydrate	6 g
Dietary Fiber	1 g
Sugars	4 g
Protein	1 g

Italian-Style Caponata

Serving Size: 1/4 cup, Total Servings: 16

2 tablespoons vegetable oil

1 large unpeeled eggplant
(about 1-1/2 pounds),
coarsely chopped

1 medium onion, chopped

2 tablespoons garlic powder

1/2 cup chopped pimiento-
stuffed green olives

3 celery ribs, chopped

1 can (8 ounces) tomato
sauce

1/4 cup white vinegar

1/3 cup packed light brown
sugar

2 to 3 dashes hot pepper
sauce (optional)

1 In a large saucepan, heat the oil
over medium-high heat. Add the
eggplant, onion, and garlic powder
and sauté for about 5 minutes, or
until the eggplant begins to soften,
stirring occasionally.

2 Stir in the remaining ingredients
and cook over medium heat for
25 minutes to allow the flavors to
marry.

3 Serve immediately or allow to cool,
then cover and chill until ready to
serve.

Exchanges
1/2 Carbohydrate
1/2 Fat

Calories	63
Calories from Fat	22
Total Fat	2 g
Saturated Fat	0 g
Cholesterol	0 mg
Sodium	191 mg
Carbohydrate	10 g
Dietary Fiber	2 g
Sugars	8 g
Protein	1 g

"This year-round
Italian-style party spread
is especially perfect for big
get-togethers. It even makes a
nice change-of-pace Christmas
Day appetizer. Chock-full of
goodness, this is really festive served over toasted
bread triangles or on
crackers."

Tex-Mex Black Bean Dip

Serving Size: 1/4 cup, Total Servings: 16

2 cans (16 ounces each) black beans, rinsed and drained, divided

1 cup salsa, divided

1 teaspoon vegetable oil

1 medium onion, finely chopped

1 medium-sized red bell pepper, finely chopped

3 garlic cloves, minced

1 tablespoon dried cilantro leaves

2 teaspoons ground cumin

1/4 teaspoon salt

1/4 cup finely shredded reduced-fat Cheddar cheese

1 medium tomato, chopped

1 In a blender or a food processor fitted with its metal cutting blade, combine 1 can beans and 1/4 cup salsa; blend or process until smooth.

2 Heat the oil in a large nonstick skillet over medium heat and sauté the onion, pepper, and garlic for 5 to 7 minutes, or until the onion and pepper are tender.

3 Add the puréed bean mixture, the cilantro, cumin, salt, and the remaining can of beans and salsa; mix well. Reduce the heat to low and simmer for about 5 minutes, stirring frequently.

4 Pour the dip into a shallow serving dish, top with the cheese and tomato, and serve immediately.

Exchanges
1/2 Starch
1 Vegetable

Calories.............................72
   Calories from Fat..............9
Total Fat.............................1 g
   Saturated Fat.....................0 g
Cholesterol..........................1 mg
Sodium...........................144 mg
Carbohydrate..................12 g
   Dietary Fiber.....................4 g
   Sugars................................2 g
Protein..............................4 g

Finishing Touch

No need to wait for Cinco de Mayo to enjoy this hearty Mexican-style dip. Serve it with baked tortilla chips and fresh veggie sticks, and dig in!

See Photo Insert

Jamaican Jerk Chicken

Serving Size: 2 strips, Total Servings: 6

2 teaspoons ground allspice

2 teaspoons dried thyme

1/2 teaspoon ground cinnamon

1/2 teaspoon garlic powder

1/2 teaspoon ground red pepper

1/2 teaspoon salt

1 pound boneless, skinless chicken breast, cut into 12 strips

2 teaspoons vegetable oil

1 In a shallow dish, combine the allspice, thyme, cinnamon, garlic powder, ground red pepper, and salt; mix well.

2 Toss the chicken strips in the mixture, turning to coat completely.

3 In a medium skillet, heat the oil over medium-high heat. Cook the chicken strips in batches, if necessary, for 2 to 3 minutes per side, or until no pink remains. Serve immediately.

Exchanges
2 Lean Meat

Calories...........................107
  Calories from Fat............32
Total Fat..............................4 g
  Saturated Fat.....................1 g
Cholesterol.......................46 mg
Sodium..............................168 mg
Carbohydrate.....................1 g
  Dietary Fiber....................0 g
  Sugars..............................0 g
Protein ....17 g

Did You Know...

that the custom of "jerking" meat, poultry, and fish is a 300-year-old Jamaican tradition used to preserve and flavor foods? Jerked foods have a spicy-sweet flavor and tender texture. My recipe doesn't take nearly as long as traditional jerk recipes, but it's still flavor-packed. And if you want to serve it with a dipping sauce, try a light ranch dressing; it really complements the intense jerk flavor.

Smoked Turkey Spread

Serving Size: 1/4 cup, Total Servings: 6

1/2 pound sliced smoked deli turkey, finely chopped

1/2 cup light mayonnaise

2 tablespoons finely chopped celery

1/4 teaspoon black pepper

1 In a medium bowl, combine all the ingredients; mix well. Serve, or cover and chill until ready to serve.

"I hope that, like me, you've long ago kicked the cigarette smoking habit—that is, if you ever started it. So, to recognize the Great American Smokeout (held each year on the 3rd Thursday of November), why not serve this spread either with crackers, on sliced cucumbers, or stuffed in hollowed-out cherry tomatoes. And when you do, remember to celebrate how lucky all of us are who are no longer tobacco dependent!"

Exchanges
1 Lean Meat
1 Fat

Calories..........................107
　Calories from Fat............62
Total Fat..............................7 g
　Saturated Fat......................1 g
Cholesterol........................27 mg
Sodium..........................529 mg
Carbohydrate.....................2 g
　Dietary Fiber....................0 g
　Sugars...............................1 g
Protein.............................7 g

Thai Beef Satay

Serving Size: 2 skewers, Total Servings: 12

24 wooden skewers

1 pound flank steak, cut into 24 thin slices

1/2 cup reduced-fat creamy peanut butter

2 tablespoons light soy sauce

2 teaspoons sesame oil

1 tablespoon butter

2 teaspoons crushed red pepper

1 Preheat the oven to 350°F. Soak the wooden skewers in water for 15 to 20 minutes. Thread the slices of beef onto the skewers and place on a rimmed baking sheet.

2 In a small saucepan, combine the remaining ingredients over low heat until melted and smooth.

3 Brush evenly over the beef skewers, completely coating them, and bake for 8 to 10 minutes, or until desired doneness.

Exchanges
1/2 Carbohydrate
1 Lean Meat
1 Fat

Calories 132
   Calories from Fat 73
Total Fat ....8 g
   Saturated Fat ....3 g
Cholesterol ....20 mg
Sodium ....192 mg
Carbohydrate ....5 g
   Dietary Fiber.....................1 g
   Sugars................................2 g
Protein ....10 g

Good for You!
Since November is American Diabetes Month and also Peanut Butter Lovers' Month, why not celebrate by making dishes with good-for-you peanut butter? It's good for almost everybody, since research suggests that including low-glycemic index foods like peanut butter as part of a healthy diet can significantly reduce the risk of type 2 diabetes.

Zesty Sausage Meatballs

Serving Size: 3 meatballs, Total Servings: 12

1 pound ground pork

1/2 cup plain bread crumbs

1/4 cup water

1 small onion, chopped

1/4 cup chopped fresh parsley

1 teaspoon crushed fennel seed

1/2 teaspoon garlic powder

1/4 teaspoon ground red pepper

1/2 teaspoon salt

1/2 teaspoon black pepper

1 Preheat the oven to 350°F. Coat a rimmed baking sheet with nonstick cooking spray. In a large bowl, combine all the ingredients; mix well. Form the mixture into 36 one-inch balls.

2 Place on the baking sheet and bake for 15 to 18 minutes, or until no pink remains, turning the meatballs over halfway through baking.

Exchanges
1 Medium-Fat Meat
1/2 Fat

Calories 99
    Calories from Fat 52
Total Fat ....6 g
    Saturated Fat ....2 g
Cholesterol ....25 mg
Sodium ....156 mg
Carbohydrate ....4 g
    Dietary Fiber ....0 g
    Sugars ....1 g
Protein ....7 g

Options

These robust-tasting meatballs are perfect for your next Super Bowl party, or for any bash. Just serve 'em with warmed spaghetti sauce for dipping. And you know what else? They work with lean ground beef, veal, and even ground turkey breast, so they can be a bit different every time you serve them.

Hot Diggity Dog "Bites"

Serving Size: 4 bites, Total Servings: 16

1/4 cup yellow mustard

2 tablespoons sweet pickle relish

Eight 6-inch flour tortillas

8 reduced-fat turkey hot dogs
(1 pound)

Toothpicks

1 Preheat the oven to 350°F. Coat a baking dish with nonstick cooking spray.

2 In a small bowl, combine the mustard and relish; mix well. Spread equally over each tortilla.

3 Place one hot dog on the edge of each tortilla, and roll up. Trim and discard the ends of the tortillas. Cut each roll into eight equal pieces and secure each with a toothpick.

4 Place the hot dog bites on the baking sheet and bake for 12 to 15 minutes, or until heated through and the tortillas are golden.

Exchanges
1/2 Starch
1 Medium-Fat Meat

Calories	108
Calories from Fat	46
Total Fat	5 g
Saturated Fat	2 g
Cholesterol	25 mg
Sodium	459 mg
Carbohydrate	11 g
Dietary Fiber	1 g
Sugars	1 g
Protein	5 g

Good for You!

With reduced-fat turkey franks having just 7.5 grams of fat each, compared to traditional beef franks with a whopping 16 grams each, this is the way to celebrate starting a new school year with a no-sacrifice, kid-pleasin' treat!

Baked Sesame Shrimp

Serving Size: 3 shrimp, Total Servings: 12 to 13

1 cup self-rising flour

1/4 teaspoon salt

1/4 teaspoon ground red pepper

3/4 cup club soda

1 pound medium shrimp
   (36 to 40 count), peeled and
   deveined with tails left on

2 teaspoons sesame seeds

Nonstick cooking spray

1 Preheat the oven to 400°F. Coat rimmed baking sheets with nonstick cooking spray.

2 In a medium bowl, combine the flour, salt, and pepper. Pour the club soda into the flour mixture and whisk until combined.

3 Holding the shrimp by the tails, dip them into the batter, coating completely. Place the shrimp about 3 inches apart on the baking sheets. The batter will puddle around each shrimp.

4 Sprinkle each shrimp with sesame seeds then coat lightly with nonstick cooking spray. Bake for 12 to 13 minutes, or until coating is golden.

Exchanges
1/2 Starch
1 Very Lean Meat

Calories	64
Calories from Fat	6
Total Fat	1 g
Saturated Fat	0 g
Cholesterol	48 mg
Sodium	239 mg
Carbohydrate	8 g
Dietary Fiber	0 g
Sugars	0 g
Protein	6 g

"When you serve this Asian favorite to kick off the Chinese New Year, I bet nobody will believe you when you tell 'em it's not fried! They'll love your dipping sauce, too, made by mixing 1/4 cup plum jelly with 2 tablespoons light soy sauce."

Garlicky Shrimp

Serving Size: 3 shrimp, Total Servings: 8 to 10

2 tablespoons butter

1 tablespoon vegetable oil

4 garlic cloves, minced

1/4 cup chopped fresh parsley

1/4 teaspoon salt

1 pound large shrimp
(24 to 30 count), peeled and
deveined

1 tablespoon fresh lemon juice

1 In a large skillet, heat the butter and oil over medium heat.

2 Add the garlic, parsley, salt, and shrimp, and sauté for 1 to 2 minutes.

3 Drizzle with the lemon juice and continue cooking until the shrimp are pink. Serve immediately.

Exchanges
1 Very Lean Meat
1 Fat

Calories 72
   Calories from Fat 40
Total Fat ....4 g
   Saturated Fat ....2 g
Cholesterol ....71 mg
Sodium ....166 mg
Carbohydrate ....1 g
   Dietary Fiber ....0 g
   Sugars................................0 g
Protein ....7 g

Did You Know...

that shrimp is the ultimate "gourmet" fast food? It cooks up in minutes and allows us to serve a fancy meal without a fancy restaurant price tag!

Festive Crab Spread

Serving Size: 1/4 cup, Total Servings: 6

1 package (8 ounces) reduced-fat cream cheese, softened

1/4 pound imitation crabmeat, flaked

1/2 teaspoon lemon juice

1 tablespoon chopped fresh dill weed

1 Preheat the oven to 350°F.

2 In a medium bowl, combine all the ingredients; mix well and spoon into a 1/2-quart baking dish.

3 Bake for 25 to 30 minutes, or until golden and heated through. Serve warm.

"It seems like crab has become a New Year's Eve favorite. If you want to continue that tradition at your house (or start a new one!), this is the way to serve it—of course, topped with a crab claw for garnish."

Exchanges
1 Lean Meat
1 Fat

Calories 112
  Calories from Fat 74
Total Fat ....8 g
  Saturated Fat ....5 g
Cholesterol ....31 mg
Sodium ....318 mg
Carbohydrate ....3 g
  Dietary Fiber ....0 g
  Sugars ....3 g
Protein ....6 g

Mini Crab Cakes

Serving Size: 2 crab cakes, Total Servings: 18

1/2 cup Italian-flavored bread crumbs

1/2 cup egg substitute

1/2 of a medium-sized red bell pepper, finely chopped

1/2 of a medium-sized red onion, finely chopped

1 rib celery, finely chopped

3 tablespoons light mayonnaise

2 teaspoons fresh lemon juice

3/4 teaspoon black pepper

1 teaspoon crushed dried tarragon

3 cans (6-1/2 ounces each) lump crabmeat, drained

2 tablespoons vegetable oil

1 In a medium bowl, combine all the ingredients except the crabmeat and oil; mix well. Fold in the crabmeat, being careful not to break up the crabmeat chunks.

2 Form the mixture into 36 equal-sized patties. Heat the oil in a large skillet over medium heat.

3 Add the patties and cook in batches for 2 to 3 minutes per side, or until golden brown. Serve warm.

Exchanges
1 Lean Meat

Calories	62
Calories from Fat	25
Total Fat	3 g
Saturated Fat	0 g
Cholesterol	19 mg
Sodium	152 mg
Carbohydrate	3 g
Dietary Fiber	0 g
Sugars	1 g
Protein	5 g

Serving Tip

Try these with a zippy sauce you can whip up from 1/4 cup light mayonnaise, 2 teaspoons prepared horseradish, 1 tablespoon ketchup, and a squeeze of fresh lemon.

Salmon Croquettes

Serving Size: 2 croquettes, Total Servings: 7

1 can (14-3/4 ounces) pink salmon, drained, bones removed, and flaked

1 egg

2 tablespoons yellow mustard

3/4 cup herb-seasoned stuffing mix

1/2 cup all-purpose flour

1/4 cup vegetable oil

1 In a large bowl, combine the salmon, egg, and mustard; mix well. Stir in the stuffing mix, and form into 14 small patties.

2 Place the flour in a shallow dish. Add the salmon patties, turning to coat completely.

3 Heat the oil in a large skillet over medium-high heat. Add the patties and cook in batches for 2 to 3 minutes per side, or until golden. Serve immediately.

"These are one of my grandmother's specialties. 'Big Mamma,' as I called her, always made these mini croquettes for appetizers at family reunions and holiday dinners."

Exchanges

1 Starch
1 Lean Meat
1-1/2 Fat

Calories 212
   Calories from Fat 108
Total Fat .... 12 g
   Saturated Fat .... 0 g
Cholesterol .... 59 mg
Sodium .... 427 mg
Carbohydrate .... 12 g
   Dietary Fiber .... 1 g
   Sugars .... 1 g
Protein .... 13 g

Smoked Salmon Pizza

Serving Size: 2 wedges, Total Servings: 8

Two 10-inch flour tortillas

4 ounces reduced-fat cream cheese, softened

2 teaspoons chopped fresh dill weed

1 package (3 ounces) smoked salmon, coarsely chopped

2 tablespoons finely chopped red onion

1 Preheat the oven to 450°F. Place the tortillas on a baking sheet.

2 In a small bowl, combine the cream cheese and dill; mix well and spread evenly over each tortilla. Sprinkle evenly with the salmon and onion.

3 Bake for 6 to 7 minutes, or until heated through and the tortilla edges are golden. Cut each into 8 wedges and serve warm.

Exchanges
1/2 Starch
1 Lean Meat
1/2 Fat

Calories...........................107
   Calories from Fat............43
Total Fat............................5 g
   Saturated Fat...................2 g
Cholesterol.....................13 mg
Sodium...........................229 mg
Carbohydrate..................11 g
   Dietary Fiber....................1 g
   Sugars..............................1 g
Protein.............................5 g

Good for You!
Choosing reduced-fat cream cheese allows us to indulge ourselves with this decadent appetizer.

Soups, Salads, and Breads

Chinese Chicken Soup

Serving Size: 1 cup, Total Servings: 10

4 cans (14 ounces each) reduced-
   sodium chicken broth

1 cup water

1 tablespoon light soy sauce

1 cup sliced fresh mushrooms

1 can (8 ounces) sliced water
   chestnuts, drained

1 can (8 ounces) sliced bamboo
   shoots, drained

1/2 pound boneless, skinless
   chicken breast, cut into
   1/2-inch chunks

1/4 pound uncooked spaghetti,
   broken in half

1 cup fresh snow peas, trimmed

2 scallions, sliced

1 In a soup pot, combine the chicken broth, water, soy sauce, mushrooms, water chestnuts, bamboo shoots, and chicken over medium-high heat and bring to a boil.

2 Add the spaghetti and snow peas, and continue boiling for 8 minutes, or until the pasta is cooked, stirring occasionally. Top each serving with sliced scallions.

Exchanges
1/2 Starch
1 Very Lean Meat
1 Vegetable

Calories............................107
   Calories from Fat..............6
Total Fat............................1 g
   Saturated Fat......................0 g
Cholesterol........................13 mg
Sodium............................451 mg
Carbohydrate....................14 g
   Dietary Fiber......................2 g
   Sugars................................3 g
Protein..............................10 g

Did You Know...

that the Chinese New Year is also known as the "spring festival"? That goes along with the belief that it is a chance to get a fresh start.

See Photo
Insert

Veggie Patch Soup

Serving Size: 1 cup, Total Servings: 10

6 cups water

2 medium-sized white potatoes, peeled and cut into 1-inch chunks

4 large tomatoes, cored and cut into 1-inch chunks

4 medium-sized carrots, peeled and cut into 1-inch chunks

3 medium-sized zucchini, cut into 1-inch chunks

2 medium-sized green bell peppers, coarsely chopped

2 medium-sized onions, coarsely chopped

3 garlic cloves, minced

1-1/2 teaspoons salt

1/2 teaspoon black pepper

1 In a soup pot, combine all the ingredients; mix well and bring to a boil over high heat.

2 Reduce the heat to medium and cook for 1 hour, or until the vegetables are tender.

"You can give this a bit of extra richness by adding a sprinkle of Parmesan cheese to the top of each serving. And remember, since Parmesan is a strong, flavorful cheese, a little goes a long way!"

Exchanges
1/2 Starch
2 Vegetable

Calories	84
Calories from Fat	4
Total Fat	0 g
Saturated Fat	0 g
Cholesterol	0 mg
Sodium	383 mg
Carbohydrate	20 g
Dietary Fiber	4 g
Sugars	7 g
Protein	2 g

Soups, Salads, and Breads

Garlic Soup

Serving Size: 1 cup, Total Servings: 8

8 garlic cloves, minced

3 cans (14 ounces each) reduced-sodium chicken broth

1-1/2 cups water

4 slices stale or toasted bread, cut into 1/2-inch cubes

1/2 teaspoon black pepper

1 egg, beaten

1 scallion, thinly sliced

1 Coat a soup pot with nonstick cooking spray.

2 Add the garlic to the pot and cook over medium heat until lightly brown, stirring constantly. Add the broth, water, bread, and pepper; mix well. Bring to a boil, then reduce the heat to low.

3 Remove 2 tablespoons of the soup to a small bowl and combine with the beaten egg. Using a fork, slowly stir the egg mixture into the soup, forming egg strands. Cook for 4 to 5 minutes, until heated through.

4 Top each serving with sliced scallions, and serve immediately.

"It's hard not being able to indulge in sweets on Halloween, so here's something festive that we can really enjoy. Not only does this taste great, but it should protect us from Halloween vampires and goblins, too!"

Exchanges
1/2 Starch

Calories 62
   Calories from Fat 10
Total Fat ....1 g
   Saturated Fat ....0 g
Cholesterol ....27 mg
Sodium ....425 mg
Carbohydrate ....8 g
   Dietary Fiber ....0 g
   Sugars ....2 g
Protein ....4 g

Spicy Black Bean Soup

Serving Size: 1 cup, Total Servings: 9

2 cans (14 ounces each) reduced-sodium beef broth

2 cups water

1 medium onion, chopped

3 cans (15 ounces each) black beans

1 jar (16 ounces) salsa

1/2 teaspoon ground cumin

1 In a soup pot, combine the broth, water, and onion over medium-high heat. Cook for 5 minutes, or until the onion is tender; reduce the heat to medium-low.

2 Meanwhile, rinse and drain 2 cans of beans and set aside. In a blender, purée the remaining can of undrained beans until smooth. Add the bean purée and the rinsed beans to the broth mixture.

3 Stir in the salsa and cumin and simmer for 5 minutes, until the soup is thoroughly heated, stirring occasionally.

4 For thick soup, simmer for an additional 20 to 30 minutes, stirring occasionally.

Exchanges
2 Starch

Calories	149
Calories from Fat	5
Total Fat	1 g
Saturated Fat	0 g
Cholesterol	0 g
Sodium	552 mg
Carbohydrate	27 g
Dietary Fiber	10 g
Sugars	5 g
Protein	10 g

Serving Tip
To celebrate the end of the workweek, serve this zippy soup topped with a swirl of reduced-fat sour cream and some chopped onion.

Fishermen's Minestrone

Serving Size: 1 cup, Total Servings: 16

3 cans (14 ounces each) reduced-
sodium beef broth

1 can (28 ounces) crushed tomatoes

1 can (19 ounces) garbanzo beans
(chick peas), undrained

1 can (15-1/4 ounces) red kidney
beans, undrained

1 package (16 ounces) frozen mixed
vegetables, thawed

1 package (16 ounces) frozen chopped
spinach, thawed and drained

1 small onion, chopped

1 teaspoon garlic powder

1/2 teaspoon black pepper

1/2 cup uncooked elbow macaroni

1 pound fresh or frozen white-fleshed
fish fillets, such as cod, haddock, or
whiting, cut into 1-inch chunks

1 pound fresh shrimp, peeled and
deveined

1. In a large soup pot, combine the broth, crushed tomatoes, garbanzo beans, kidney beans, mixed vegetables, spinach, onion, garlic powder, and pepper. Bring to a boil over high heat.

2. Stir in the macaroni and cook for 8 minutes, or until the macaroni is tender.

3. Reduce the heat to low, add the fish and shrimp, and simmer for 5 to 7 minutes, or until the fish flakes easily with a fork and the shrimp turn pink, stirring occasionally.

Exchanges
1 Starch
1 Very Lean Meat
2 Vegetable

Calories	166
Calories from Fat	10
Total Fat	1 g
Saturated Fat	0 g
Cholesterol	48 mg
Sodium	561 mg
Carbohydrate	24 g
Dietary Fiber	5 g
Sugars	6 g
Protein	15 g

Good for You!

What could be better than a "beat the mid-winter blues" soup that not only tastes great, but is chock-full of veggies and seafood? This one really packs an extra-nutritious punch, since the spinach and fish contain omega fatty acids, which help our bodies maintain healthy cholesterol levels and have been shown to reduce the risk of heart attack and stroke.

Creamy Spinach Soup

Serving Size: 1 cup, Total Servings: 7

8 scallions, thinly sliced

1 teaspoon minced garlic

2 cans (14 ounces each) vegetable broth

2 packages (10 ounces each) frozen spinach, thawed and well drained

3 tablespoons cornstarch

3 cups low-fat (1%) milk

1/2 teaspoon ground nutmeg

1/2 teaspoon salt

1/4 teaspoon black pepper

1 Coat a soup pot with nonstick cooking spray.

2 Add the scallions and garlic to the pot and sauté over medium heat for 3 to 4 minutes, or until tender. Stir in the broth and spinach. Cover, and reduce the heat to low; simmer for 20 minutes.

3 In a small bowl, combine the cornstarch and milk; stir until the cornstarch is dissolved. Pour into the soup and stir until well combined.

4 Add the remaining ingredients to the soup and cook, stirring constantly, for 6 to 8 minutes, or until the soup thickens. Serve immediately.

Did You Know...

that by using low-fat milk instead of traditional heavy cream, we've reduced the calories by two-thirds, but kept all the smooth flavor?!

Exchanges
1 Carbohydrate

Calories	93
Calories from Fat	14
Total Fat	2 g
Saturated Fat	1 g
Cholesterol	4 mg
Sodium	499 mg
Carbohydrate	16 g
Dietary Fiber	3 g
Sugars	6 g
Protein	6 g

Hot-and-Sour Soup

Serving Size: 1 cup, Total Servings: 5

2 cans (14 ounces each) reduced-sodium chicken broth, divided

2 tablespoons cornstarch

1/2 pound firm tofu, cut into small chunks

1/4 pound sliced fresh mushrooms

2 tablespoons light soy sauce

3 tablespoons white vinegar

1 teaspoon ground ginger

1 teaspoon black pepper

1 egg, lightly beaten

1 cup fresh bean sprouts

1/2 teaspoon sesame oil

1 In a small bowl, combine 1/4 cup chicken broth and the cornstarch; mix well and set aside.

2 In a soup pot, combine the remaining chicken broth, the tofu, mushrooms, soy sauce, vinegar, ginger, and pepper; mix well and bring to a boil over high heat. Reduce the heat to low; stir in the cornstarch mixture until thickened.

3 Slowly stir in the beaten egg to form egg strands.

4 Add the bean sprouts and simmer for 1 to 2 minutes, or until heated through, stirring occasionally. Add the sesame oil; mix well and serve.

Exchanges
1/2 Carbohydrate
1 Lean Meat

Calories............................89
Calories from Fat............26
Total Fat............................3 g
Saturated Fat....................1 g
Cholesterol......................43 mg
Sodium..........................644 mg
Carbohydrate....................8 g
Dietary Fiber....................1 g
Sugars............................3 g
Protein............................8 g

Good for You!

Instead of putting a whole bowl of crispy fried noodles on the table to tempt you, just sprinkle a few on top of each bowl right before serving.

Cool Cucumber Soup

Serving Size: 1 cup, Total Servings: 5

4 large cucumbers, peeled, seeded, and chopped

1 container (16 ounces) low-fat plain yogurt

1 garlic clove

1 tablespoon chopped fresh dill weed

1 teaspoon salt

1 In a blender or a food processor fitted with its metal cutting blade, purée all the ingredients until smooth, scraping down the sides of the container as necessary.

2 Transfer to a large bowl, cover, and chill for at least 2 hours, or overnight. Serve chilled.

"This is so cool and satisfying that you feel like you're cheating on your meal plan … but you aren't, so enjoy! Oh—for an extra-sweet touch, sometimes I add a tablespoon of honey to the ingredients before processing."

Exchanges
1 Carbohydrate

Calories	82
Calories from Fat	15
Total Fat	2 g
Saturated Fat	1 g
Cholesterol	7 mg
Sodium	533 mg
Carbohydrate	12 g
Dietary Fiber	1 g
Sugars	10 g
Protein	6 g

Strawberry Patch Soup

Serving Size: 3/4 cup, Total Servings: 7

2 packages (16 ounces each) frozen strawberries with no added sugar, thawed

1 can (12 ounces) frozen apple juice concentrate, thawed

2 tablespoons sugar

1 teaspoon vanilla extract

1/2 cup water

1 tablespoon cornstarch

1 cup reduced-fat sour cream

1 In a medium saucepan, combine the strawberries, apple juice concentrate, sugar, and vanilla extract over medium heat. Bring to a boil, reduce the heat to low, and cook for 5 minutes, stirring occasionally.

2 In a small bowl, combine the water and cornstarch, stirring until smooth. Add the cornstarch mixture to the soup pot and stir constantly for 1 minute, or until thick and clear. Allow to cool, then pour into a blender or a food processor and purée for 5 to 10 seconds, or until the mixture is smooth and frothy.

3 Transfer to a large bowl, cover, and chill for at least 2 hours before serving. Just before serving, stir in the sour cream.

Exchanges
3 Fruit
1/2 Fat

Calories	206
Calories from Fat	29
Total Fat	3 g
Saturated Fat	2 g
Cholesterol	11 mg
Sodium	39 mg
Carbohydrate	43 g
Dietary Fiber	3 g
Sugars	38 g
Protein	3 g

"When we think of soup, we usually think 'hot.' Well, not this one! This cool, creamy fruit soup is the perfect opening act for summer brunches and get-togethers. It's especially appropriate for bridal showers and weddings if you consider the Cherokee belief that strawberries are a symbol of good luck!"

Zesty Marinated Salad

Serving Size: 1 cup, Total Servings: 11

4 cups broccoli florets

1 small zucchini, cut into 1-inch chunks

1 small yellow squash, cut into 1-inch chunks

1 medium-sized red bell pepper, cut into 1-inch chunks

1 small red onion, cut into 1/2-inch chunks

1/2 pint cherry tomatoes, halved

3/4 cup low-fat Italian dressing

1/4 cup balsamic vinegar

2 tablespoons honey

1 In a large bowl, combine the broccoli, zucchini, yellow squash, pepper, onion, and tomatoes.

2 In a small bowl, combine the remaining ingredients; mix well. Pour over the vegetable mixture; toss until well coated. Cover and chill for at least 2 hours before serving.

Exchanges
1/2 Carbohydrate
1 Vegetable

Calories............................56
  Calories from Fat............12
Total Fat...........................1 g
  Saturated Fat.....................0 g
Cholesterol.........................0 mg
Sodium............................271 mg
Carbohydrate...................11 g
  Dietary Fiber.....................2 g
  Sugars...............................8 g
Protein...............................2 g

Good for You!
Salad dressing is an easy instant marinade for our veggies, but instead of creamy varieties, use vinegar-based ones to add flavor without fat.

Mardi Gras Gumbo, page 66

Tex-Mex Black Bean Dip, page

Almond Fudge Brownies, page 178

Creamy Pumpkin Mousse, page 176

Oven-"Fried" Drumsticks, page 67
Mexican Corn Bread, page 145
Apple Cider Slaw, page 153

Strawberry Spinach Salad

Serving Size: 1 cup, Total Servings: 10

1 package (10 ounces) fresh baby spinach, washed, dried, and trimmed

1 pint fresh strawberries, cleaned and sliced lengthwise to 1/4-inch thickness

1/2 of a small onion, finely chopped

2 tablespoons sugar

3 tablespoons water

2 tablespoons white vinegar

1/2 teaspoon dry mustard

1/4 cup canola or vegetable oil

1 Place the spinach in a large salad bowl; add the strawberries.

2 In a small bowl, combine the onion, sugar, water, vinegar, mustard, and oil. Whisk until well combined.

3 Drizzle the dressing over the salad and toss to coat. Serve immediately.

Exchanges
1/2 Carbohydrate
1 Fat

Calories............................79
Calories from Fat............53
Total Fat..............................6 g
Saturated Fat......................0 g
Cholesterol..........................0 mg
Sodium..............................23 mg
Carbohydrate....................6 g
Dietary Fiber....................2 g
Sugars..............................4 g
Protein................................1 g

Serving Tip

What a perfect salad to celebrate spring! And if you need to make it in advance ... no problem! Just prepare the spinach, strawberries, and dressing separately, and keep everything chilled in individual containers until ready to toss and serve.

Farm Stand Salad

Serving Size: 1 cup, Total Servings: 10

1/2 cup vegetable oil

1/2 cup apple cider vinegar

1 tablespoon finely chopped fresh dill weed

1 teaspoon salt

1 teaspoon black pepper

1/2 pound fresh green beans, trimmed, cooked, and chilled

6 radishes, thinly sliced

1 medium-sized head iceberg lettuce, torn into bite-sized pieces

1 large tomato, cut into 1-inch chunks

1 medium-sized green bell pepper, cut into 1-inch chunks

1 large cucumber, thinly sliced

1 small onion, finely chopped

6 hard-boiled eggs, cut into wedges

1 In a small bowl, whisk the oil, vinegar, dill, salt, and black pepper until well combined.

2 Place the remaining ingredients except the eggs in a large serving bowl; toss lightly. Arrange the egg wedges on top; drizzle the salad with the dressing, and serve immediately.

Exchanges
2 Vegetable
3 Fat

Calories............................177
   Calories from Fat..........131
Total Fat...........................15 g
   Saturated Fat.....................1 g
Cholesterol......................128 mg
Sodium...........................279 mg
Carbohydrate....................7 g
   Dietary Fiber.....................2 g
   Sugars...............................3 g
Protein..............................5 g

Finishing Touch

There's no doubt about it, we eat with our eyes. So, for a change of pace from traditional tossed salads, why not arrange all these ingredients in a colorful pattern on a platter and drizzle with the dressing. Boy, will everybody's eyes light up as you set this on the table!

Caesar Salad

Serving Size: 1 cup, Total Servings: 12

1/2 cup light mayonnaise

1/3 cup low-fat (1%) milk

1-1/2 teaspoons Dijon-style mustard

1 tablespoon lemon juice

1/4 cup grated Parmesan cheese

1/4 teaspoon garlic powder

1/4 teaspoon salt

1/4 teaspoon black pepper

1 large head romaine lettuce, washed and torn into bite-sized pieces

1 In a medium bowl, combine all the ingredients except the romaine; whisk until smooth and creamy.

2 Place the romaine in a large salad bowl and toss with the dressing. Serve immediately.

Exchanges
1 Vegetable
1 Fat

Calories	55
Calories from Fat	38
Total Fat	4 g
Saturated Fat	1 g
Cholesterol	6 mg
Sodium	193 mg
Carbohydrate	2 g
Dietary Fiber	0 g
Sugars	1 g
Protein	2 g

Great Go-Alongs
If you want this to be like the authentic Caesar salad, top it with croutons—but in moderation. Simply toss cubed day-old bread with a bit of garlic powder, salt, and pepper, then toast in a 300°F. oven until golden.

Special Seven-Layer Salad

Serving Size: 1/8 recipe, Total Servings: 8

1 head romaine lettuce, washed, dried, and chopped

3 medium tomatoes, chopped and seeded

3 carrots, chopped

2 celery stalks, chopped

1 package (10 ounces) frozen green peas, thawed

3/4 cup Smooth 'n' Creamy Dressing, divided (see recipe on opposite page)

1/2 pound low-fat turkey bacon, cooked and crumbled

6 hard-boiled eggs, peeled and chopped

1 cup (4 ounces) shredded Italian cheese blend

1. In a large glass salad or trifle bowl, combine the romaine lettuce and tomatoes. In a medium-sized bowl, combine the carrots and celery, then layer over the lettuce and tomato mixture. In the same medium-sized bowl, combine the peas with 1/4 cup dressing; mix well and layer over the carrots and celery.

2. Sprinkle with the crumbled turkey bacon, then layer with the hard-boiled eggs, followed by the shredded cheese. Drizzle with the remaining 1/2 cup dressing and serve, or cover and chill until ready to serve.

Exchanges
1/2 Starch
2 Medium-Fat Meat
1 Vegetable
1 Fat

Calories..........................265
    Calories from Fat..........149
Total Fat..........................17 g
    Saturated Fat....................6 g
Cholesterol....................195 mg
Sodium..........................684 mg
Carbohydrate..................14 g
    Dietary Fiber....................4 g
    Sugars..............................7 g
Protein............................16 g

"This special salad is a celebration in and of itself. Not only is it delicious, it's beautiful. That makes this the perfect main dish for any get-together."

Smooth 'n' Creamy Dressing

Serving Size: 2 tablespoons, Total Servings: 8

1/2 cup light mayonnaise

1/4 cup fat-free (skim) milk

2 tablespoons white vinegar

1 tablespoon Dijon mustard

1/4 teaspoon onion powder

1/4 teaspoon garlic powder

1/4 teaspoon black pepper

1 In a medium bowl, whisk together all the ingredients until smooth.

2 Serve, or cover and chill until ready to serve.

"This one's perfect for April Fool's Day, 'cause nobody's gonna believe this creamy, smooth dressing is made from light ingredients! A drizzle of this on any salad, and you'll feel richly indulged."

Exchanges
1 Fat

Calories 55
   Calories from Fat 46
Total Fat ....5 g
   Saturated Fat ....1 g
Cholesterol ....5 mg
Sodium ....169 mg
Carbohydrate ....2 g
   Dietary Fiber ....0 g
   Sugars ....1 g
Protein ....1 g

Crunchy Sesame Breadsticks

Serving Size: 1 breadstick, Total Servings: 16

1 pound frozen bread dough, thawed

1/2 cup all-purpose flour

1 egg, beaten

2 tablespoons grated Parmesan cheese

1 teaspoon garlic powder

2 tablespoons sesame seeds

1 Preheat the oven to 350°F. Coat a baking sheet with nonstick cooking spray.

2 Cut the thawed dough into sixteen 1/2-inch-thick slices. Lightly flour a cutting board and, with your hands, roll out each piece of dough to about 10 inches long.

3 Place the dough sticks on the baking sheet. Brush each with the beaten egg.

4 In a small bowl, combine the remaining ingredients and sprinkle over the dough sticks. Bake for 15 to 20 minutes, or until golden.

Exchanges
1 Starch
1/2 Fat

Calories	106
Calories from Fat	20
Total Fat	2 g
Saturated Fat	1 g
Cholesterol	14 mg
Sodium	184 mg
Carbohydrate	18 g
Dietary Fiber	1 g
Sugars	1 g
Protein	4 g

"When I was growing up, I couldn't wait to be invited to our Italian neighbors' for Sunday dinner. The smells and tastes were so comforting. I'll never forget sitting in their dining room, dunking warm, soft sesame breadsticks into rich, home-made tomato sauce. Even though my version starts with prepared dough (so they're ready in no time), to this day, when I taste these, I feel like a kid again."

Yorkshire Pudding Popovers

Serving Size: 1 popover, Total Servings: 6

2 eggs, well chilled

1 cup cold low-fat (1%) milk

1 tablespoon butter, melted

1 cup all-purpose flour

2 scallions, thinly sliced

1/2 teaspoon garlic powder

1/2 teaspoon salt

1 Preheat the oven to 425°F. Coat a 6-cup muffin tin with nonstick cooking spray.

2 In a large bowl, combine all the ingredients and beat with a wooden spoon until smooth. Immediately pour the batter into the muffin cups.

3 Bake for 30 to 35 minutes, or until golden and puffy.

4 Cool slightly before removing from the muffin cups. Serve immediately.

Exchanges
1 Starch
1 Fat

Calories............................137
    Calories from Fat............38
Total Fat.............................4 g
    Saturated Fat.....................2 g
Cholesterol........................78 mg
Sodium............................256 mg
Carbohydrate..................19 g
    Dietary Fiber.....................1 g
    Sugars...............................2 g
Protein..............................6 g

Great Go-Along
Yorkshire pudding takes its name from a northern county of England where it became a popular go-along for roast beef in the 1700s. Today it's more often made like a popover than as a pudding, and my version is very easy to make. So don't wait for a special occasion to enjoy this ... Yorkshire pudding makes any occasion feel like a holiday!

Onion Board

Serving Size: 2 squares, Total Servings: 12

2 tablespoons butter

1 medium onion, diced

1 pound frozen bread dough, thawed

1 egg, beaten

1/2 teaspoon poppy seeds

1 Preheat the oven to 350°F. Coat a large rimmed baking sheet with non-stick cooking spray.

2 In a medium skillet, melt the butter and cook the onion over medium heat for 6 to 8 minutes, or until the onion is soft and lightly browned.

3 On a lightly floured surface, roll out the dough to a 10" × 15" rectangle. With your fingertips, gently spread the dough to cover the pan, and push it up to the edges of the pan, forming a rim. If the dough is too sticky, dust it and your hands lightly with flour.

4 Brush the dough with the beaten egg, then spread the cooked onion evenly over the top. Sprinkle with the poppy seeds and bake for 25 to 30 minutes, or until golden.

5 Remove to a cutting board; let cool slightly, then cut into squares.

Exchanges
1-1/2 Starch
1/2 Fat

Calories............................130
   Calories from Fat............33
Total Fat.............................4 g
   Saturated Fat......................2 g
Cholesterol........................23 mg
Sodium..............................244 mg
Carbohydrate...................20 g
   Dietary Fiber.....................1 g
   Sugars...............................2 g
Protein...............................4 g

Serving Tip
Just wait till you hear all the thanks you'll be getting on Easter, Thanksgiving, and any time this shows up in your bread basket. It's a great one to make ahead of time, so, if you do, just throw it in a 300°F. oven to warm for 5 minutes before serving.

Cinnamon Apple Flat Bread

Serving Size: 2 squares, Total Servings: 12

1 pound frozen bread dough, thawed

1/4 cup peach all-fruit spread

4 medium apples, cored, peeled, and thinly sliced

1 tablespoon sugar

1 teaspoon ground cinnamon

1 Preheat the oven to 350°F. Coat a large rimmed baking sheet with nonstick cooking spray.

2 On a lightly floured surface, roll out the dough to a 10" × 15" rectangle. With your fingertips, gently spread the dough to cover the pan, and push it up to the edges of the pan, forming a rim. If the dough is too sticky, dust it and your hands lightly with flour.

3 Spread the fruit spread over the dough, then top with the sliced apples, arranged in a single layer.

4 In a small bowl, combine the sugar and cinnamon. Sprinkle over the apples. Bake for 20 to 25 minutes, or until the edges are golden.

5 Remove from the oven and cool slightly in the pan on a wire rack. Slice, and serve warm.

Exchanges
2 Carbohydrate

Calories	143
Calories from Fat	13
Total Fat	1 g
Saturated Fat	0 g
Cholesterol	0 mg
Sodium	221 mg
Carbohydrate	29 g
Dietary Fiber	2 g
Sugars	11 g
Protein	3 g

"When the apple orchards are overflowing, that's the perfect time to take advantage of the season's best. And this one's such a treat that I couldn't decide if it belonged with the breads or desserts. What do you think?"

Saucy Banana Bread

Serving Size: 1 slice, Total Servings: 12 slices

1 cup sugar

3/4 cup unsweetened applesauce

2 eggs

2 cups all-purpose flour

1 teaspoon baking soda

1/2 teaspoon salt

1 cup mashed ripe bananas
(about 3 medium bananas)

1 teaspoon vanilla extract

1 Preheat the oven to 350°F. Coat a 9" × 5" loaf pan with nonstick cooking spray.

2 In a large bowl, cream together the sugar and applesauce with an electric beater on medium-high speed. Add the eggs and beat thoroughly. Gradually add the flour, baking soda, and salt, blending well. Beat in the mashed bananas and vanilla extract until well combined.

3 Pour the batter into the loaf pan. Bake for 55 to 60 minutes, or until light golden.

4 Immediately remove from the pan and place on a wire rack to cool.

Exchanges
2-1/2 Carbohydrate

Calories............................174
Calories from Fat............10
Total Fat..............................1 g
Saturated Fat....................0 g
Cholesterol........................36 mg
Sodium............................213 mg
Carbohydrate...................38 g
Dietary Fiber....................1 g
Sugars.............................21 g
Protein..............................3 g

Good for You!

Whether we have diabetes or not, we all should eat foods that are good for us. And wait until you taste this! The traditional oil is replaced with applesauce, which makes an incredible difference in calories, yet keeps the bread moist as can be!

Studded Cranberry Loaf

Serving Size: 1 slice, Total Servings: 12

1/4 cup egg substitute

1/4 cup vegetable oil

1 cup sugar

3/4 cup orange juice

1/2 cup walnuts

1 cup fresh or frozen cranberries, thawed

2 cups all-purpose flour

1-1/2 teaspoons baking powder

1/2 teaspoon baking soda

1/2 teaspoon salt

1 Preheat the oven to 350°F. Coat a 9" × 5" loaf pan with nonstick cooking spray.

2 In a food processor fitted with its metal cutting blade, combine the egg substitute, oil, sugar, orange juice, walnuts, and cranberries. Pulse until the nuts and cranberries are coarsely chopped.

3 In a large bowl, combine the flour, baking powder, baking soda, and salt. Add the cranberry mixture and stir just until the mixture is moistened and blended.

4 Pour the batter into the loaf pan and bake for 50 to 60 minutes, or until golden on top and a wooden toothpick inserted in the center comes out clean. Cool in the pan on a wire rack.

Exchanges
1 Carbohydrate
1-1/2 Fat

Calories............................225
   Calories from Fat............72
Total Fat.............................8 g
   Saturated Fat.....................0 g
Cholesterol.........................0 mg
Sodium............................206 mg
Carbohydrate...................36 g
   Dietary Fiber.....................1 g
   Sugars.............................19 g
Protein................................3 g

Good for You!

"I love breads and everything else that's loaded with carbohydrates, so this is my kind of treat—especially with the cranberries giving it its tangy kick. This is great for Christmas morning and other special times, but be wise about your portions, because this will count as a major part of your daily allowance of carbs."

Poultry

Lemon Rosemary Chicken

Serving Size: 1/5 of recipe, Total Servings: 5

1 whole chicken
   (about 3 pounds)

1 tablespoon chopped fresh parsley

1 tablespoon dried rosemary

1/2 teaspoon rubbed sage

1/2 teaspoon salt

1/4 teaspoon black pepper

1 lemon, cut in half

1 tablespoon vegetable oil

1 teaspoon paprika

1 Preheat the oven to 350°F. Place the chicken on a roasting rack in a roasting pan.

2 In a medium bowl, combine the parsley, rosemary, sage, salt, and pepper. Using your fingertips, gently lift the skin from the chicken breasts, without detaching it, and rub the seasoning mixture over the breast meat.

3 Squeeze the lemon juice over the chicken, then place the lemon shells inside the chicken cavity. Rub the chicken with the oil, then sprinkle with the paprika.

4 Cover the chicken with aluminum foil and roast for 1 hour. Remove the foil and bake for 25 to 30 more minutes, or until no pink remains in the chicken and its juices run clear.

Good for You!

When we're watching what we eat, it makes sense to pass on the gravy and simply make dishes like this where fresh herbs and lemon are more than enough to excite our taste buds.

Exchanges
Without Skin
3 Lean Meat

Calories	167
Calories from Fat	59
Total Fat	7 g
Saturated Fat	2 g
Cholesterol	77 mg
Sodium	307 mg
Carbohydrate	0 g
Dietary Fiber	0 g
Sugars	0 g
Protein	25 g

Exchanges
With Skin
4 Medium-Fat Meat

Calories	285
Calories from Fat	155
Total Fat	17 g
Saturated Fat	4 g
Cholesterol	94 mg
Sodium	322 mg
Carbohydrate	1 g
Dietary Fiber	0 g
Sugars	0 g
Protein	29 g

French Country Chicken

Serving Size: 1 breast half, Total Servings: 4

4 boneless, skinless chicken breast halves (about 1 pound total), pounded to 1/2-inch thickness

1/2 cup seasoned bread crumbs

4 slices Muenster cheese

1/4 cup dry white wine

1 Preheat the oven to 350°F. Coat a 9" × 13" baking dish with nonstick cooking spray.

2 Coat the chicken with the bread crumbs, turning to coat completely. Place in the baking dish and bake for 15 minutes.

3 Remove the chicken from the oven, top with the cheese, and pour the wine evenly over the top.

4 Bake for 15 minutes, or until no pink remains in the chicken and the cheese is bubbly and golden.

Exchanges
1 Starch
4 Lean Meat

Calories	298
Calories from Fat	106
Total Fat	12 g
Saturated Fat	6 g
Cholesterol	96 mg
Sodium	638 mg
Carbohydrate	12 g
Dietary Fiber	1 g
Sugars	1 g
Protein	33 g

"Vive la France! Yes, the traditional French pairing of wine and cheese in this dish makes it a Bastille Day favorite, but be advised: Cheese sometimes adds to your carbohydrate ratio. If you count correctly, you can enjoy all the wonderful varieties of foods you can get your hands on. I know ... because I do!"

Tomato–Wine Chicken

Serving Size: 1/5 of recipe, Total Servings: 5

1 can (8 ounces) tomato sauce

1 can (4 ounces) mushroom stems and pieces, drained

1/2 cup dry white wine

1 onion, chopped

1 garlic clove, minced

1/4 teaspoon salt

1/4 teaspoon black pepper

1 chicken (about 3 pounds), cut into 10 pieces and skin removed

2 tablespoons water

1 tablespoon all-purpose flour

1 In a soup pot, combine the tomato sauce, mushrooms, wine, onion, garlic, salt, and pepper over medium heat. Add the chicken, stirring to coat completely. Bring to a low boil.

2 Reduce the heat to low, cover, and simmer for 45 minutes, or until no pink remains in the chicken and its juices run clear. Remove the chicken to a platter and cover to keep warm.

3 In a small bowl, combine the water and flour; mix well and stir into the sauce. Simmer over low heat for 1 to 2 minutes, or until the sauce thickens. Serve the chicken topped with the sauce.

Exchanges
1/2 Carbohydrate
3 Lean Meat

Calories 207
   Calories from Fat 60
Total Fat ....7 g
   Saturated Fat ....2 g
Cholesterol ....77 mg
Sodium ....522 mg
Carbohydrate ....8 g
   Dietary Fiber ....1 g
   Sugars ....4 g
Protein ....27 g

Did You Know...
that a good part of the alcohol content of wine is absorbed in cooking? That means that, in moderation, we can enjoy the flavorful taste it adds to our cooked recipes.

Mardi Gras Gumbo

Serving Size: Approximately 1-1/2 cups, Total Servings: 10

1 pound boneless, skinless chicken breasts, cut into 1-inch chunks

1 pound boneless, skinless chicken thighs, cut into 1-inch chunks

1 can (28 ounces) diced tomatoes, undrained

1 can (15-1/4 ounces) whole-kernel corn, drained

1 package (16 ounces) frozen cut okra, thawed

2 cans (14 ounces each) reduced-sodium chicken broth

1 tablespoon hot pepper sauce

1/2 teaspoon liquid smoke

1 teaspoon black pepper

1. In a soup pot, combine all the ingredients over high heat and bring to a boil.

2. Reduce the heat to medium and simmer for 40 to 45 minutes, or until no pink remains in the chicken and the gumbo thickens, stirring occasionally.

Exchanges
1/2 Starch
3 Very Lean Meat
1 Vegetable

Calories	163
Calories from Fat	26
Total Fat	3 g
Saturated Fat	1 g
Cholesterol	63 mg
Sodium	478 mg
Carbohydrate	11 g
Dietary Fiber	2 g
Sugars	4 g
Protein	23 g

Serving Tip

This "festive as a Mardi Gras parade" soup needs just a small scoop of cooked rice to help us sop up its flavorful juices. That's all we need to satisfy us— without overdoing the carbs!

See Photo Insert

Oven-"Fried" Drumsticks

Serving Size: 2 drumsticks, Total Servings: 4

1/4 cup all-purpose flour

1 egg

1/4 cup low-fat (1%) milk

1 cup coarsely crushed oven-
  toasted corn cereal

1/2 teaspoon dried oregano

1/2 teaspoon garlic powder

1/2 teaspoon onion powder

1/2 teaspoon paprika

1/2 teaspoon dried basil

1/2 teaspoon salt

1/4 teaspoon black pepper

8 chicken drumsticks, skin
  removed

Nonstick cooking spray

1 Preheat the oven to 375°F. Coat a rimmed baking sheet with nonstick cooking spray.

2 Place the flour in a shallow dish. In a second shallow dish, beat the eggs with the milk. In a third shallow dish, mix the crushed cereal with the seasonings.

3 Dip the chicken in the flour, then into the egg mixture, then into the cereal mixture, coating evenly with each. Arrange the chicken on the baking sheet and coat with nonstick cooking spray.

4 Bake for 25 minutes, then turn the chicken and bake for 25 more minutes, or until no pink remains in the chicken and it turns golden.

Exchanges
1 Starch
3 Lean Meat

Calories	247
Calories from Fat	59
Total Fat	7 g
Saturated Fat	2 g
Cholesterol	132 mg
Sodium	498 mg
Carbohydrate	17 g
Dietary Fiber	1 g
Sugars	2 g
Protein	28 g

Serving Tip

Cook up a batch of this crunchy chicken and pair it with coleslaw and a green salad for an indoor midwinter picnic. Simply spread a blanket on the floor, light a fire in the fireplace or turn up the thermostat, get out your summer duds, and let the party begin!

See Photo Insert

Chicken Stroganoff

Serving Size: 1/6 recipe, Total Servings: 6

1 small onion, chopped

1/2 pound fresh mushrooms, sliced

1-1/2 pounds boneless, skinless chicken breasts, cut into thin strips

1 can (10-3/4 ounces) reduced-fat condensed cream of mushroom soup

1/2 cup dry white wine

1/8 teaspoon black pepper

1/2 cup reduced-fat sour cream

2 tablespoons chopped fresh parsley

1/2 pound no-yolk egg noodles, cooked according to package directions, drained, rinsed, drained again, and kept warm

1. In a large skillet, sauté the onions and mushrooms over high heat for 5 minutes, or until the onions are tender. Add the chicken strips and sauté for 5 minutes.

2. Add the soup, wine, and black pepper; mix well. Reduce the heat to medium and cook for 5 minutes, or until the sauce appears smooth and no pink remains in the chicken, stirring occasionally.

3. Add the sour cream and parsley and cook for 1 minute, or until the sour cream is blended; do not boil. Serve over the warm cooked noodles.

"Holiday or not, I'm a real poultry lover! I look forward to making turkey on Thanksgiving, Cornish hens on Valentine's Day, and this one any day I have a reason to celebrate!"

Exchanges
2-1/2 Starch
3 Very Lean Meat
1 Fat

Calories............................349
Calories from Fat............58
Total Fat..............................6 g
Saturated Fat......................2 g
Cholesterol........................77 mg
Sodium............................473 mg
Carbohydrate..................36 g
Dietary Fiber......................3 g
Sugars..................................5 g
Protein..............................33 g

Chicken à l'Orange

Serving Size: 1/5 of recipe, Total Servings: 5

1 chicken (about 3 pounds), cut into 10 pieces and skin removed

1/2 teaspoon salt

1/2 cup orange marmalade

1 can (11 ounces) mandarin oranges, drained

1/8 teaspoon ground red pepper

1. Preheat the oven to 350°F. Coat a 9" × 13" baking dish with nonstick cooking spray.

2. Place the chicken in the baking dish. Season with the salt and bake for 35 minutes; drain liquid from the baking dish.

3. In a small bowl, combine the remaining ingredients then pour over the chicken.

4. Bake uncovered for 20 to 25 minutes, or until no pink remains in the chicken and its juices run clear.

Exchanges
1-1/2 Carbohydrate
3 Lean Meat

Calories	258
Calories from Fat	59
Total Fat	7 g
Saturated Fat	2 g
Cholesterol	77 mg
Sodium	326 mg
Carbohydrate	25 g
Dietary Fiber	1 g
Sugars	18 g
Protein	26 g

"Even though she had a different name for it, my grandmother loved making this dish. Now, when I think about the ingredients, I bet I finally know why! Grandma was oh-so sweet, and Grandpa was spicy-hot ... hot-tempered, I mean. If that sounds like any of *your* relatives, then this might be just the fun dish to serve on National Grandparents Day (always the first Sunday after Labor Day), or any other special day."

Spanish Chicken

Serving Size: 1 chicken breast half with 3/4 cup rice, Total Servings: 4

1 tablespoon vegetable oil

4 boneless, skinless chicken breast halves (1 pound total)

1 medium-sized onion, diced

1 medium-sized green bell pepper, diced

1-1/2 cups instant brown rice

1 cup chicken broth

1 can (14-1/2 ounces) diced tomatoes, undrained

1 teaspoon dried thyme

1/4 teaspoon crushed red pepper

1/4 teaspoon salt

1/2 teaspoon black pepper

1. In a large skillet, heat the oil over medium heat. Add the chicken breasts and brown for 5 minutes on each side. Remove from the skillet and set aside.

2. Add the onion and bell pepper to the skillet and sauté over medium heat for 5 to 6 minutes, or until tender. Return the chicken to the skillet and add the rice, chicken broth, tomatoes, thyme, red and black peppers, and salt; stir until well combined.

3. Cover and simmer over medium-low heat for 10 minutes, or until no pink remains in the chicken. Turn off the heat, cover the skillet, and let sit for 5 minutes. Fluff rice and serve.

Exchanges
2 Starch
3 Very Lean Meat
2 Vegetable
1 Fat

Calories............................357
  Calories from Fat............71
Total Fat...........................8 g
  Saturated Fat.....................1 g
Cholesterol........................69 mg
Sodium..............................671 mg
Carbohydrate...................42 g
  Dietary Fiber....................4 g
  Sugars...............................7 g
Protein.............................31 g

"Nothing beats this dish when it comes to savory comfort. I keep this one in mind for welcoming the gang home when the weather starts to cool off!"

Sesame-Crusted Chicken

Serving Size: 1 breast half, Total Servings: 6

1/2 cup all-purpose flour

2 eggs, beaten

1/2 cup Italian-seasoned bread crumbs

1/4 cup sesame seeds

2 teaspoons dried thyme

1 teaspoon garlic powder

1/2 teaspoon salt

1/4 teaspoon black pepper

6 boneless, skinless chicken breast halves (1-1/2 pounds total), pounded to 1/2-inch thickness

2 tablespoons vegetable oil

1 Place the flour in a shallow dish and the eggs in another shallow dish; in a third shallow dish, combine the bread crumbs, sesame seeds, thyme, garlic powder, salt, and pepper; mix well.

2 Dip the chicken into the flour, then the eggs, then the bread crumb mixture, coating evenly with each.

3 In a large skillet, heat the oil over medium heat. Sauté the chicken in batches for 4 minutes per side, or until no pink remains.

Exchanges
1 Starch
4 Lean Meat

Calories............................314	
Calories from Fat..........116	
Total Fat ....13 g	
Saturated Fat ....2 g	
Cholesterol......................139 mg	
Sodium ....419 mg	
Carbohydrate..................17 g	
Dietary Fiber.....................2 g	
Sugars...............................1 g	
Protein ....31 g	

Did You Know...

that the sesame seed was the first recorded seasoning, dating back to 3000 BC? Its slightly sweet, nutty flavor is still popular today as it flavors and fancies up loads of dishes.

Mom's Chicken Cordon Bleu

Serving Size: 1 breast half, Total Servings: 6

2 slices (2 ounces) deli ham, coarsely chopped

1/2 cup (2 ounces) shredded Swiss cheese

6 boneless, skinless chicken breast halves (about 1-1/2 pounds total)

1/2 teaspoon salt

1/2 teaspoon black pepper

1 tablespoon Italian bread crumbs

1/8 teaspoon paprika

1 Preheat the oven to 350°F. Coat a 6-cup muffin tin with nonstick cooking spray.

2 In a small bowl, combine the ham and cheese; mix well and set aside.

3 Between 2 pieces of wax paper, gently pound the chicken with a mallet or rolling pin to 1/4-inch thickness. Season the chicken breasts with salt and pepper, then place equal amounts of the ham and cheese mixture in the center of each and roll up tightly, tucking in the sides as you roll.

4 Place the rolls seam side down in the cups of the muffin tin. Sprinkle with bread crumbs and paprika.

5 Bake for 25 to 30 minutes, or until no pink remains in the chicken and its juices run clear. Serve immediately.

Exchanges
4 Very Lean Meat
1 Fat

Calories	189
Calories from Fat	54
Total Fat	6 g
Saturated Fat	3 g
Cholesterol	82 mg
Sodium	412 mg
Carbohydrate	1 g
Dietary Fiber	0 g
Sugars	0 g
Protein	30 g

"The muffin tins make this recipe such a cinch that it's easy to impress Mom with your 'fancy French-cooking skills' on Mother's Day. Of course, now that you know the trick, you won't want to reserve it for just one day a year!"

Chicken Marsala

Serving Size: 1 breast half, Total Servings: 6

1/4 cup all-purpose flour

6 boneless, skinless chicken
    breast halves (1-1/2 pounds
    total), pounded to 1/4-inch
    thickness

2 tablespoons butter

2 tablespoons olive oil

1/2 pound fresh mushrooms,
    sliced

1/4 teaspoon salt

1/4 teaspoon black pepper

3/4 cup Marsala wine

1 Place the flour in a shallow dish. Add the chicken and coat evenly; set aside.

2 In a large skillet, heat the butter and oil over medium heat. Cook the chicken in batches for 3 to 4 minutes per side, or until golden and no pink remains. Remove the cooked chicken to a platter and keep warm.

3 Add the mushrooms to the skillet; sprinkle with salt and pepper, and sauté for 3 to 5 minutes, or until tender. Return the chicken to the skillet, add the wine, and reduce the heat to low.

4 Cook for 3 to 5 minutes, or until the sauce thickens and the chicken is heated through. Serve immediately.

Exchanges
1/2 Carbohydrate
4 Very Lean Meat

Calories	256
Calories from Fat	98
Total Fat	11 g
Saturated Fat	4 g
Cholesterol	78 mg
Sodium	199 mg
Carbohydrate	8 g
Dietary Fiber	1 g
Sugars	2 g
Protein	26 g

Did You Know...

that October 16 is Boss's Day? Why not show your appreciation by treating the boss to a homemade fancy tasting meal like this, and who knows? Maybe you'll end up with a corner office!

Chicken Piccata

Serving Size: 1 breast half, Total Servings: 4

1/4 cup all-purpose flour

1 egg, lightly beaten

4 boneless, skinless chicken
  breast halves (1 pound total),
  pounded to 1/4-inch thickness

1/4 teaspoon salt

1/4 teaspoon black pepper

2 tablespoons butter

1/3 cup dry white wine

1 tablespoon capers

1 lemon, cut in half

1 Place the flour in a shallow dish.
Place the beaten egg in another
shallow dish. Season the chicken
with salt and pepper. Coat the
chicken breasts with the flour, then
dip in the egg.

2 In a large skillet, melt the butter
over medium-high heat. Cook the
chicken for 3 to 4 minutes per side,
until golden.

3 Add the wine and capers to the skillet and squeeze the lemon over the
chicken. Cook for 2 to 4 more minutes, or until the chicken is cooked
through and the sauce begins to
glaze the chicken.

Exchanges
1/2 Carbohydrate
4 Lean Meat

Calories 243
  Calories from Fat 89
Total Fat .... 10 g
  Saturated Fat .... 5 g
Cholesterol .... 137 mg
Sodium .... 346 mg
Carbohydrate .... 7 g
  Dietary Fiber .... 0 g
  Sugars .... 1 g
Protein .... 28 g

"Pounding the
chicken so thin
makes this cook up in
no time—which means
that even if you get last-
minute guests, they'll
think you fussed
for hours!"

Nicole's Famous Chicken

Serving Size: 1 chicken breast half and sauce, Total Servings: 6

6 boneless, skinless chicken breast halves (1-1/2 pounds total)

1/2 pound fresh mushrooms, sliced

1 medium-sized green bell pepper, chopped

1 small onion, minced

1 can (10-3/4 ounces) condensed reduced-fat cream of mushroom soup

1 Coat a large skillet with nonstick cooking spray and heat over medium heat.

2 Add the chicken, mushrooms, pepper, and onion to the skillet; brown the chicken for 3 minutes per side while sautéing the vegetables.

3 Add the soup; reduce the heat to medium-low, cover, and cook until no pink remains in the chicken, and the sauce is bubbly. Serve the chicken topped with the sauce.

"I love making this dish—it's so easy and delicious! I remember my grandmother making it when I was young and, once I was diagnosed with diabetes, we just added more veggies and eliminated the rice she used to serve with it. See, you don't need to give up all your family favorites. As Mr. Food says (but in Spanish) ... 'Ooh es muy bueno!'"

Exchanges
1/2 Carbohydrate
4 Very Lean Meat

Calories	185
Calories from Fat	40
Total Fat	4 g
Saturated Fat	1 g
Cholesterol	70 mg
Sodium	439 mg
Carbohydrate	9 g
Dietary Fiber	2 g
Sugars	3 g
Protein	27 g

Apple-Glazed Turkey

Serving Size: 1/16 turkey, Total Servings: 16

One 12- to 14-pound turkey

1 teaspoon salt

1/2 teaspoon black pepper

2 apples, cored and quartered

1 container (12 ounces) frozen
  apple juice concentrate,
  thawed

1 can (14 ounces) ready-to-use
  chicken broth

1-1/2 teaspoons rubbed sage

1 Preheat the oven to 325°F. Line a
  roasting pan with aluminum foil.

2 Place the turkey in the roasting pan
  and rub it inside and out with the
  salt and pepper; place the apples
  inside the cavity. Pour the apple
  juice concentrate evenly over the
  turkey. Pour the chicken broth into
  the pan.

3 Sprinkle the sage evenly over the
  top of the turkey. Cover loosely
  with aluminum foil and roast for
  3 hours, basting with the pan juices
  every 30 minutes.

4 Remove the foil and roast for
  another 1 to 1-1/2 hours, or until no
  pink remains in the turkey and its
  juices run clear. Allow to sit for
  15 minutes before carving.

Exchanges
1 Carbohydrate
7 Lean Meat

Calories 432
  Calories from Fat 162
Total Fat ....18 g
  Saturated Fat ....6 g
Cholesterol ....147 mg
Sodium ....384 mg
Carbohydrate ....14 g
  Dietary Fiber ....0 g
  Sugars...............................13 g
Protein ....51 g

Change of Pace

This and the recipe on the
next page will ensure that your
Thanksgiving turkey is filled
with so much flavorful pizzazz
that you won't even need to
worry about fixing gravy. Just
drain the fat from their natural juices and serve that
as a light sauce.

Champagne-Roasted Turkey

Serving Size: 2 to 3 slices, Total Servings: 12

One 7-pound bone-in turkey breast

1/2 pound red seedless grapes, stemmed and cut in half (about 1-1/2 cups), divided

1/2 teaspoon salt

1/2 teaspoon black pepper

1 bottle (750 ml) champagne (see Change of Pace)

1 can (14 ounces) ready-to-use chicken broth

2 tablespoons cornstarch

1 Preheat the oven to 350°F. Line a roasting pan with aluminum foil and coat with nonstick cooking spray.

2 Place the turkey in the pan and spoon 1 cup grape halves into the neck cavity. Season the turkey all over with the salt and pepper. Pour the champagne into the pan around the turkey.

3 Roast the turkey for 2-1/4 to 2-1/2 hours, or until no pink remains and its juices run clear, basting every 30 minutes with the pan juices. If the turkey begins to get too browned, cover loosely with aluminum foil.

4 In a medium saucepan, combine the chicken broth, cornstarch, and the pan drippings with the fat removed; bring to a boil over medium-high heat, stirring constantly until thickened. Stir in the remaining 1/2 cup grape halves and cook for 1 to 2 minutes, or until heated through.

5 Carve the turkey and serve with the champagne-grape sauce.

Exchanges
1/2 Carbohydrate
7 Very Lean Meat

Calories............................272
   Calories from Fat............49
Total Fat..............................5 g
   Saturated Fat......................1 g
Cholesterol.......................147 mg
Sodium............................334 mg
Carbohydrate.....................5 g
   Dietary Fiber......................0 g
   Sugars................................3 g
Protein ....48 g

Change of Pace
This year, to fancy up that holiday bird, try bathing it in champagne as in this recipe, or even using nonalcoholic sparkling wine or cider. It's a simple but fancy way out of the "plain old roasted turkey" rut!

Garlic-Crusted Cornish Hens

Serving Size: 1/2 Cornish hen, Total Servings: 8

2 tablespoons olive oil

1 teaspoon dried oregano

1 teaspoon dried basil

1/2 teaspoon salt

1 teaspoon black pepper

4 Cornish hens (about 1 pound each)

16 cloves garlic, coarsely chopped

1 Preheat the oven to 350°F. Coat a roasting pan with nonstick cooking spray.

2 In a small bowl, combine the oil, oregano, basil, salt, and pepper; mix well.

3 Place the Cornish hens in the roasting pan. Place the garlic evenly over the hens, then spoon the oil mixture over them.

4 Roast uncovered for 1-1/4 to 1-1/2 hours, or until no pink remains in the hens and their juices run clear, basting every 20 minutes.

5 Cut each hen in half before serving.

Exchanges
4 Medium-Fat Meat
1 Fat

Calories	353
Calories from Fat	228
Total Fat	25 g
Saturated Fat	7 g
Cholesterol	161 mg
Sodium	225 mg
Carbohydrate	2 g
Dietary Fiber	0 g
Sugars	2 g
Protein	28 g

Did You Know...

that these are also known as Rock Cornish game hens? They're simply miniature chickens weighing between 1 and 2 pounds. If they're not available in the fresh meat case, you should find them in the frozen foods section.

Turkey Cacciatore Meatballs

Serving Size: 3 meatballs, Total Servings: 8

1 pound ground turkey breast

1/2 cup Italian-flavored bread crumbs

1/2 cup grated Parmesan cheese

1/2 of a medium-sized green bell pepper, finely chopped

1/2 of a medium-sized onion, finely chopped

1 jar (28 ounces) light spaghetti sauce, divided

2 eggs

2 teaspoons garlic powder

1 teaspoon dried oregano

1/2 teaspoon black pepper

1/4 cup olive oil

1 In a large bowl, combine the turkey, bread crumbs, Parmesan cheese, bell pepper, onion, 1/4 cup spaghetti sauce, the eggs, garlic powder, oregano, and black pepper. With clean hands, combine the mixture until thoroughly mixed. Form into 24 meatballs; set aside.

2 In a large pot, heat the oil over medium-high heat. Place the meatballs in the pot a few at a time and brown for 2 to 3 minutes, gently turning to brown on all sides.

3 Drain off excess liquid and add the remaining spaghetti sauce to the pot; reduce the heat to low, cover, and simmer for 18 to 20 minutes, or until the meatballs are cooked through.

Exchanges
1 Carbohydrate
3 Lean Meat

Calories............................239
   Calories from Fat............93
Total Fat...........................10 g
   Saturated Fat.....................4 g
Cholesterol........................96 mg
Sodium............................748 mg
Carbohydrate...................16 g
   Dietary Fiber.....................3 g
   Sugars...............................7 g
Protein.............................22 g

"Keep this healthier-but-still-yummy alternative in mind for those busy school nights when everybody is on the run. These cook up hot 'n' hearty in less than 30 minutes!"

Stuffed Turkey Cutlets

Serving Size: 1 turkey cutlet, Total Servings: 8

2 cups corn bread stuffing

1 can (8 ounces) water chestnuts, drained and chopped

2/3 cup hot water

2 tablespoons butter, melted

4 tablespoons chopped fresh parsley, divided

1/2 teaspoon onion powder

8 turkey breast cutlets (about 2 pounds total), slightly pounded

1 jar (12 ounces) turkey gravy

1 Preheat the oven to 350°F. Coat a 9" × 13" baking dish with nonstick cooking spray.

2 In a large bowl, combine the stuffing, water chestnuts, hot water, butter, 2 tablespoons parsley, and the onion powder; mix well.

3 Place the turkey cutlets on a work surface; place an equal amount of the stuffing mixture in the center of each and roll up tightly.

4 Place the rolls seam side down in the baking dish and cover with the gravy. Cover tightly with aluminum foil and bake for 50 to 55 minutes, or until no pink remains in the turkey.

5 Sprinkle with the remaining 2 table-spoons parsley and serve.

Exchanges
1 Starch
4 Very Lean Meat
1/2 Fat

Calories 241
  Calories from Fat 44
Total Fat ....5 g
  Saturated Fat ....2 g
Cholesterol........................78 mg
Sodium ....454 mg
Carbohydrate....................17 g
  Dietary Fiber....................2 g
  Sugars...............................2 g
Protein ....30 g

Change of Pace
No matter the time of year, turkey is always in style, and here's an easy way to bring those comforting Thanksgiving flavors to your table—even on a breezy summer night!

Meats

Bistro Steak

Serving Size: 1/6 recipe, Total Servings: 6

1-1/2 pounds 1-inch-thick bone-less beef top sirloin steak

2 tablespoons light mayonnaise

1 tablespoon Dijon-style mustard

1 teaspoon dried tarragon

1/4 teaspoon black pepper

1 Preheat the broiler. Coat a broiler pan or rimmed baking sheet with nonstick cooking spray. Place the steak on the broiler pan.

2 In a small bowl, combine the remaining ingredients; mix well. Spread the mixture over the steak, coating well.

3 Broil for 12 to 15 minutes for medium-rare, or to desired done-ness beyond that, turning halfway through the cooking. Thinly slice and serve.

Exchanges

3 Lean Meat

Calories	158
Calories from Fat	60
Total Fat	7 g
Saturated Fat	2 g
Cholesterol	66 mg
Sodium	149 mg
Carbohydrate	1 g
Dietary Fiber	0 g
Sugars	0 g
Protein	22 g

Did You Know...

that dining "al fresco" is simply dining outdoors, which in many traditional restaurants in France is the "bistro" style of dining? Why not try it at home? (It sounds fancy, doesn't it?!)

Filet Mignon au Vin

Serving Size: 1 steak and 1/2 cup sauce, Total Servings: 2

Two 1-inch-thick beef tenderloin steaks (6 ounces each)

1/4 teaspoon salt, divided

1/4 teaspoon black pepper, divided

2 teaspoons butter

1/2 of a small onion, minced

1 clove garlic, minced

1/2 pound fresh mushrooms, thinly sliced

1/4 cup dry red wine

1 Coat a large skillet with nonstick cooking spray. Season the steaks with 1/8 teaspoon salt and 1/8 teaspoon pepper.

2 Heat the skillet over medium heat. Add the steaks and cook for 6 to 8 minutes per side, or to desired doneness. Remove from the skillet; set aside and keep warm.

3 Melt the butter in the skillet over medium-high heat; add the onion, garlic, mushrooms, and the remaining 1/8 teaspoon each of salt and pepper; sauté the mushrooms and onion until tender.

4 Stir in the wine and cook over medium-high heat for 4 to 5 minutes, or until the wine is reduced by half. Serve the steaks topped with the mushroom-wine sauce.

Exchanges
4 Lean Meat
2 Vegetable
1 Fat

Calories	309
Calories from Fat	133
Total Fat	15 g
Saturated Fat	7 g
Cholesterol	100 mg
Sodium	404 mg
Carbohydrate	8 g
Dietary Fiber	2 g
Sugars	4 g
Protein	33 g

"You, your darling, your beef fillets in mushroom-wine sauce, candles, music, romance ... sounds like a recipe for a fabulous Valentine's Day celebration."

Sautéed Sirloin Tips

Serving Size: 1/6 recipe, Total Servings: 6

4 tablespoons (1/2 stick) butter, divided

1 large onion, sliced

4 garlic cloves, minced, divided

2 tablespoons chopped fresh parsley, divided

1 package (8 ounces) sliced fresh mushrooms

1 large zucchini, cut into 1/4-inch slices

1-1/2 pounds boneless beef top sirloin steak, cut into thin strips

1/4 teaspoon salt

1/4 teaspoon black pepper

2 tablespoons dry sherry (optional)

1 In a large skillet, melt 2 tablespoons butter over medium heat. Add the onion, half the minced garlic, and 1 tablespoon chopped parsley; cook for 5 to 6 minutes, or until the onion is golden.

2 Add the mushrooms and zucchini and cook for 5 minutes, or until tender, stirring constantly. Remove the vegetable mixture from the skillet and set aside.

3 Season the steak with the salt and pepper. Add the remaining 2 tablespoons butter to the skillet and melt over medium-high heat. Add the steak and the remaining minced garlic and 1 tablespoon chopped parsley; cook for 5 minutes, or to desired degree of doneness, stirring constantly.

4 Return the vegetable mixture to the skillet and stir in the sherry, if desired. Cook until heated through, stirring constantly.

Exchanges
3 Lean Meat
1 Vegetable
1 Fat

Calories 240
   Calories from Fat 115
Total Fat ....13 g
   Saturated Fat ....7 g
Cholesterol ....84 mg
Sodium ....229 mg
Carbohydrate ....7 g
   Dietary Fiber ....2 g
   Sugars ....4 g
Protein ....24 g

Good for You!

Beef is a great source of protein, and it fits into a healthy diet if we eat it in moderation. Check page 11 for my "Portion Pointers."

Twin Pepper Steak Kabobs

Serving Size: 1 kabob, Total Servings: 8

Eight 10- to 12-inch metal or wooden skewers

1 cup ketchup

1/4 cup steak sauce

1/2 cup packed light brown sugar

1/2 cup apple cider vinegar

2 tablespoons Worcestershire sauce

2 pounds boneless beef top sirloin steak, well trimmed and cut into 32 equal-sized chunks

1 medium-sized green bell pepper, cut into 16 pieces

1 medium-sized red bell pepper, cut into 16 pieces

1 In a medium saucepan, combine the ketchup, steak sauce, brown sugar, vinegar, and Worcestershire sauce over medium heat; bring to a boil, stirring occasionally until the sugar is dissolved. Remove from the heat and allow marinade to cool.

2 Thread each skewer alternately with 4 pieces of steak, 2 pieces of green pepper, and 2 pieces of red pepper. Place the skewers in a 9" × 13" glass baking dish and pour the cooled marinade over them. Cover and chill for at least 2 hours, or overnight.

3 Preheat the broiler to high. Coat a rimmed baking sheet with nonstick cooking spray.

4 Place the kabobs on the baking sheet, discarding any excess marinade, and broil for 14 to 16 minutes, or to desired doneness, turning halfway through the cooking.

Exchanges
1 Carbohydrate
3 Lean Meat

Calories............................198
   Calories from Fat............46
Total Fat.............................5 g
   Saturated Fat.......................2 g
Cholesterol........................64 mg
Sodium............................325 mg
Carbohydrate....................15 g
   Dietary Fiber......................1 g
   Sugars...............................10 g
Protein..............................23 g

"These sizzlers fit any time we want the big taste of the grill— 'cause they work in the broiler just as well as on the barbecue grill."

Meats

Party Tenderloin

Serving Size: 1 slice, Total Servings: 8

2 pounds beef tenderloin, trimmed

1 teaspoon onion powder

1 teaspoon garlic powder

1/2 teaspoon black pepper

1/2 teaspoon salt

1 Preheat the oven to 350°F. Coat a large, rimmed baking sheet with nonstick cooking spray and place the tenderloin on the baking sheet.

2 In a small bowl, combine the remaining ingredients and rub over the beef.

3 Cook for 35 to 40 minutes for medium-rare, or until desired doneness beyond that.

4 Remove the beef to a cutting board and slice across the grain into 3/4-inch slices.

Exchanges
3 Lean Meat

Calories	152
Calories from Fat	63
Total Fat	7 g
Saturated Fat	3 g
Cholesterol	60 mg
Sodium	191 mg
Carbohydrate	0 g
Dietary Fiber	0 g
Sugars	0 g
Protein	20 g

"When we want to pull out all the stops—to honor the graduate, celebrate that special birthday or anniversary, or just show how much we care—nothing beats the simple elegance of a tender, juicy tenderloin."

Valentine's Veal

Serving Size: 1/4 recipe, Total Servings: 4

1/4 cup all-purpose flour

1 egg, beaten

1 pound veal cutlets, pounded to 1/4-inch thickness

2 tablespoons butter

1 can (14 ounces) artichokes, drained and chopped

1/4 cup sun-dried tomatoes, reconstituted and chopped

1/3 cup dry vermouth or white wine

Juice of 1 lemon

1 Place the flour and egg in separate shallow dishes. Coat the veal with flour, then egg.

2 In a large skillet, melt the butter over medium heat. Cook the veal in batches for 2 to 3 minutes per side, or until golden.

3 Stir in the artichokes, sun-dried tomatoes, vermouth, and lemon juice. Cook for 2 to 3 minutes, or until the sauce thickens. Serve immediately.

Exchanges
1 Carbohydrate
3 Medium-Fat Meat

Calories............................299
   Calories from Fat..........117
Total Fat............................13 g
   Saturated Fat.....................6 g
Cholesterol......................159 mg
Sodium...........................308 mg
Carbohydrate...................13 g
   Dietary Fiber.....................1 g
   Sugars..............................3 g
Protein.............................30 g

Change of Pace

Whether you're sharing Valentine's Day dinner with the kids or another couple, this fancy dish, laden with artichokes and sun-dried tomatoes, is sure to melt your sweetie's heart! (And if you happen to be dining alone—of course by candlelight—then just wrap up the two extra portions to enjoy all over again the next evening!)

See Photo, opposite page

Valentine's Veal, page 88
Beet Mashed Potatoes, page 135
Herbed Asparagus, page 154

Chinese Chicken Soup, page 39

Clams Pomodoro, page 114

Greek Spinach Pie, page 119

Creamy Basil Pork Chops, page 89
Roasted Plum Tomatoes, page 147

Creamy Basil Pork Chops

Serving Size: 1 chop, Total Servings: 6

3 tablespoons olive oil, divided

4 garlic cloves, minced

Six 1/2-inch-thick pork loin chops (2 pounds total), well trimmed

2 tablespoons chopped fresh basil

1/4 teaspoon salt

1/4 teaspoon black pepper

1/3 cup heavy cream

1 In a large skillet, heat 2 tablespoons olive oil over medium-high heat. Add the garlic and sauté for 1 to 2 minutes. Reduce the heat to medium, add the pork chops, and cook for 6 to 7 minutes per side, until brown on both sides.

2 Meanwhile, in a small bowl, combine the remaining 1 tablespoon olive oil, the basil, salt, and pepper. Add to the skillet 3 to 4 minutes before the chops are done, spreading the mixture around the skillet and turning the chops to coat with the basil mixture. When the chops are cooked through, remove to a serving plate and cover to keep warm.

3 Whisk the cream into the pan drippings for 2 to 3 minutes over medium heat, until the sauce thickens slightly. Pour the sauce over the cooked chops and serve immediately.

Exchanges
3 Medium-Fat Meat
1/2 Fat

Calories	252
Calories from Fat	156
Total Fat	17 g
Saturated Fat	6 g
Cholesterol	81 mg
Sodium	150 mg
Carbohydrate	1 g
Dietary Fiber	0 g
Sugars	1 g
Protein	22 g

See Photo, opposite page

"October is National Pork Month, and the perfect time to go 'hog wild' over the creamy herb sauce that makes every mouthful of these juicy chops pure heaven. These are so good, everybody will think you must be cheating!"

Shortcut Stuffed Cabbage

Serving Size: 1 cup, Total Servings: 12

1-1/4 pounds ground beef

1/2 cup dry bread crumbs

1 egg

1 teaspoon salt

1/4 teaspoon black pepper

1 medium head green cabbage, shredded (12 to 14 cups)

1 can (16 ounces) whole-berry cranberry sauce

1 jar (28 ounces) light spaghetti sauce

1 tablespoon lemon juice

5 gingersnap cookies, crumbled

1. In a medium bowl, combine the ground beef, bread crumbs, egg, salt, and pepper. Using about 1 tablespoon of the mixture for each, form the mixture into 1-inch meatballs.

2. Place half of the shredded cabbage in a large pot, then add the meatballs. Spoon the cranberry sauce over the meatballs, then add the remaining cabbage. Pour the spaghetti sauce over the mixture; DO NOT STIR.

3. Bring the mixture to a boil, then reduce the heat to low and simmer uncovered for 20 minutes. Stir gently, being careful not to break up the meatballs. Simmer for 25 more minutes.

4. Add the lemon juice and cookie crumbs; mix well, and simmer for 15 more minutes.

Exchanges
2 Carbohydrate
1 Medium-Fat Meat
1 Fat

Calories	262
Calories from Fat	99
Total Fat	11 g
Saturated Fat	4 g
Cholesterol	53 mg
Sodium	627 mg
Carbohydrate	30 g
Dietary Fiber	4 g
Sugars	21 g
Protein	12 g

Change of Pace

This makes a hearty warm-you-up main dish, and a great appetizer, too. It's so good, and so easy, that there's no reason to reserve it just for special occasions.

Korean Marinated Beef

Serving Size: 4 to 5 slices, Total Servings: 4

1 medium onion, diced

1/2 cup light soy sauce

1/4 cup sugar

4 garlic cloves, minced

1/4 cup water

2 tablespoons sesame oil

4 scallions, sliced

1 tablespoon sesame seeds

1/4 teaspoon black pepper

One 1-pound flank steak

1 In a large resealable plastic storage bag, combine all the ingredients except the steak; mix well.

2 Score the steak on both sides by making shallow diagonal cuts 1 inch apart. Place the steak in the bag, seal, and marinate in the refrigerator for at least 3 hours, or overnight.

3 Remove the steak from the bag, discarding the marinade. Heat a large skillet over high heat and cook the steak for 5 to 6 minutes per side for medium-rare, or until desired doneness beyond that. Thinly slice and serve.

Exchanges
1/2 Carbohydrate
3 Lean Meat

Calories...........................217
   Calories from Fat............98
Total Fat..........................11 g
   Saturated Fat.....................4 g
Cholesterol........................54 mg
Sodium...........................470 mg
Carbohydrate.....................6 g
   Dietary Fiber.....................0 g
   Sugars...............................6 g
Protein.............................22 g

"This Asian recipe has brought new life to my cooking. Now don't be too worried that there's a bit of sugar in here. Remember, the trick for us is counting those carbohydrates correctly."

Light Spaghetti & Meatballs

Serving Size: 1 cup spaghetti and 2 meatballs, Total Servings: 8

1 pound lean ground beef

1 egg

1/2 of a small green bell pepper, finely chopped

2 tablespoons grated Parmesan cheese

1 teaspoon dried oregano

1/2 teaspoon salt

1/2 of a small onion, chopped

1 teaspoon minced garlic

1 jar (26 ounces) light spaghetti sauce

1 pound whole wheat spaghetti

1 In a large bowl, combine the ground beef, egg, pepper, Parmesan cheese, oregano, and salt; mix well and form into 16 meatballs.

2 Coat a soup pot with nonstick cooking spray. Add the meatballs and brown with the onion and garlic over medium-high heat for 8 to 10 minutes, stirring occasionally.

3 Add the spaghetti sauce and bring to a boil, stirring occasionally. Reduce the heat to medium-low and simmer for 15 to 20 minutes, or until no pink remains in the beef, stirring occasionally.

4 Meanwhile, prepare the spaghetti according to the package directions; drain. Serve the meatballs and sauce over the spaghetti.

Exchanges
3 Starch
1 Medium-Fat Meat
1 Vegetable
1-1/2 Fat

Calories	405
Calories from Fat	124
Total Fat	14 g
Saturated Fat	6 g
Cholesterol	70 mg
Sodium	699 mg
Carbohydrate	52 g
Dietary Fiber	7 g
Sugars	8 g
Protein	22 g

Good for You!

Celebrate double the light! Once our clocks "spring forward" in April, it's great to take a good-for-us, pre-dinner walk. And while we're doing it, we can look forward to this "lightened up" family favorite. Yup, this dish has significant calorie savings because we use whole wheat pasta and light spaghetti sauce instead of their traditional versions.

Sweet-and-Sour Pork Roast

Serving Size: 3 thin slices, Total Servings: 6

1/4 cup honey

2 tablespoons Dijon mustard

1/2 teaspoon salt

One 2-pound boneless center-cut single pork loin

1 Preheat the oven to 375°F. Coat a medium roasting pan with nonstick cooking spray.

2 In a medium bowl, combine the honey, mustard, and salt. Place the pork in the roasting pan and coat completely with the honey mixture.

3 Cover the pork with aluminum foil and roast for 40 minutes. Uncover and baste with the pan drippings.

4 Roast the pork uncovered for 15 to 20 more minutes, or until no pink remains. Slice and serve with the pan drippings.

Exchanges
1 Carbohydrate
3 Lean Meat

Calories...........................228
   Calories from Fat............51
Total Fat.............................6 g
   Saturated Fat.....................2 g
Cholesterol........................86 mg
Sodium...........................377 mg
Carbohydrate..................12 g
   Dietary Fiber.....................0 g
   Sugars...........................12 g
Protein............................32 g

Change of Pace
With well-trimmed pork loin being so low in fat—as low as chicken breast, and with even less cholesterol!—don't forget about "the other white meat" for a change of of pace.

Parisian Pork Medallions

Serving Size: 2 slices, Total Servings: 4

One 1-pound pork tenderloin, cut into 1-inch-thick slices

1/4 teaspoon salt

1/4 teaspoon black pepper

1 tablespoon vegetable oil

1/4 cup half-and-half

1 tablespoon Dijon mustard

1 Place the pork slices between 2 sheets of heavy-duty plastic wrap and, using a meat mallet or rolling pin, flatten to 1/4-inch thickness. Season with the salt and pepper.

2 In a large skillet, heat the oil over medium-high heat. Add the pork and cook for about 2 minutes per side, or until browned.

3 Reduce the heat to low and add the half-and-half and mustard, stirring until well combined. Serve the pork topped with the sauce.

Exchanges
3 Lean Meat
1/2 Fat

Calories............................194
   Calories from Fat............86
Total Fat..........................10 g
   Saturated Fat....................2 g
Cholesterol......................70 mg
Sodium..............................290 mg
Carbohydrate.....................2 g
   Dietary Fiber...................0 g
   Sugars................................1 g
Protein.............................25 g

Did You Know...

that fancy-sounding medallions of meat are really just round or oval pieces of meat that are either cut or pounded thin? Medallions cook up fast, which makes them perfect for an impromptu dinner party ... and talk about tender!

Balsamic Pork

Serving Size: 5 slices, Total Servings: 4

2 large red onions, thinly sliced

One 1-pound pork tenderloin

1/2 cup balsamic vinegar

1/2 cup apple juice

1/4 teaspoon salt

1/4 teaspoon black pepper

1 Coat a large skillet or wok with nonstick cooking spray; sauté the onion slices over high heat for 10 minutes, or until caramelized.

2 Spread the onions to the edge of the skillet and place the tenderloin in the center. Pour the vinegar and apple juice over the tenderloin and onions, and sprinkle with the salt and pepper. Cover and cook over medium-low heat for 10 minutes, or until desired doneness, turning the tenderloin once during cooking.

3 Thinly slice the tenderloin and serve with the caramelized onions.

Exchanges
1-1/2 Carbohydrate
3 Very Lean Meat

Calories..........................213
 Calories from Fat............39
Total Fat ....4 g
 Saturated Fat ....1 g
Cholesterol......................65 mg
Sodium ....197 mg
Carbohydrate...................20 g
 Dietary Fiber....................2 g
 Sugars..............................14 g
Protein ....25 g

Did You Know...

that the unique flavor of balsamic vinegar comes from years of aging in a series of barrels made of a wide variety of flavoring woods? It is a long process that yields this sweet yet sharp, spicy yet mellow-flavored vinegar that now has countless uses. Once you've tried balsamic vinegar, you'll agree that its classic flavor is worth all that effort!

Homestyle Veal Fricassee

Serving Size: 1/8 recipe, Total Servings: 8

2 pounds veal stew meat, well trimmed

1 large onion, chopped

1/2 cup dry white wine

6 medium carrots, cut into 1/2-inch chunks

2 beef bouillon cubes

2 bay leaves

1/4 teaspoon dried thyme

1/2 teaspoon salt

1/2 teaspoon black pepper

1/2 cup low-fat (1%) milk

1/4 cup all-purpose flour

2 teaspoons browning and seasoning sauce

1/2 pound fresh mushrooms, sliced

1 Preheat the oven to 325°F.

2 In a 3-quart covered casserole dish, combine the veal, onion, wine, carrots, bouillon cubes, bay leaves, thyme, salt, and pepper; mix well. Cover and bake for 2 hours.

3 In a small bowl, whisk together the milk, flour, and browning and seasoning sauce until no lumps remain. Slowly pour into the casserole dish, stirring constantly until thickened.

4 Stir in the mushrooms and bake uncovered for 20 to 30 more minutes, or until the mushrooms are tender. **Be sure to remove the bay leaves before serving.**

Exchanges
1 Carbohydrate
3 Very Lean Meat

Calories	189
Calories from Fat	29
Total Fat	3 g
Saturated Fat	1 g
Cholesterol	96 mg
Sodium	507 mg
Carbohydrate	13 g
Dietary Fiber	2 g
Sugars	5 g
Protein	26 g

Serving Tip

Serve this over a bit of orzo (fine, rice-like pasta) to sop up all the gravy that fricassee is known for! And remember that moderation is key when it comes to carbs, so go easy on the orzo.

Veal Oscar

Serving Size: 1 cutlet, Total Servings: 6

1/2 cup all-purpose flour

1/2 teaspoon salt

1/4 teaspoon black pepper

6 veal cutlets (about 1 pound total), lightly pounded

2 tablespoons vegetable oil, divided

1 package (10 ounces) frozen asparagus spears, thawed and drained

1 can (6-1/2 ounces) lump crabmeat, drained and flaked

1/4 cup reduced-fat sour cream

1/4 cup light mayonnaise

2 teaspoons yellow mustard

1 teaspoon fresh lemon juice

1. Preheat the oven to 450°F. In a shallow dish, combine the flour, salt, and pepper; mix well. Coat the veal in the flour mixture.

2. In a large skillet, heat 1 tablespoon oil over medium heat. Add the veal in batches and sauté for 1 to 2 minutes, or until light golden, turning once and adding additional oil as needed. Place the veal in a single layer in a 9" × 13" baking dish.

3. Top each cutlet with an equal amount of asparagus and then crab meat. In a small bowl, combine the remaining ingredients; mix well and spoon evenly over the crabmeat.

4. Bake for 8 to 10 minutes, or until bubbly and light golden. Serve immediately.

Exchanges
1 Carbohydrate
3 Lean Meat
1/2 Fat

Calories	268
Calories from Fat	119
Total Fat	13 g
Saturated Fat	3 g
Cholesterol	86 mg
Sodium	410 mg
Carbohydrate	12 g
Dietary Fiber	1 g
Sugars	1 g
Protein	25 g

"You know what I love best about this dish? The CRAB! That's because I lived in Virginia (where I won the Miss Virginia title before being crowned Miss America), where crab and other fresh seafood is plentiful. I easily incorporated it into many of my favorite recipes, and this one was always perfect for entertaining."

Beefy Pot Roast

Serving Size: 2 slices, Total Servings: 8

1/4 cup all-purpose flour

1/2 teaspoon black pepper

One 2-1/2-pound beef bottom round roast, trimmed

2 tablespoons vegetable oil

4 cups plus 1 tablespoon water, divided

2 beef bouillon cubes

2 ribs celery, chopped

1 medium onion, chopped

1 tablespoon cornstarch

1/2 teaspoon browning and seasoning sauce

1 In a shallow dish, combine the flour and pepper; mix well.

2 Rinse the beef and place in the flour mixture while still wet, turning to coat completely. In a large pot, heat the oil over medium-high heat. Add the beef and cook for 5 to 7 minutes, turning to brown on all sides.

3 Add 4 cups water, the bouillon cubes, celery, and onion. Bring to a boil, cover, and cook for 1-1/2 to 2 hours, or until the beef is fork-tender. Remove beef to a platter and keep warm.

4 In a small bowl, combine the remaining 1 tablespoon water and the cornstarch; mix well. Skim and discard the fat from the pan juices. Add the cornstarch mixture and the browning and seasoning sauce to the juices and cook for 1 to 2 minutes, or until the sauce thickens.

5 Slice the roast across the grain and serve topped with the sauce.

Exchanges
1/2 Starch
4 Lean Meat

Calories 234
   Calories from Fat 90
Total Fat .... 10 g
   Saturated Fat .... 2 g
Cholesterol .... 80 mg
Sodium .... 278 mg
Carbohydrate .... 7 g
   Dietary Fiber .... 1 g
   Sugars .... 2 g
Protein .... 27 g

Did You Know...

that pot roast is the perfect kind of roast for our slow cookers? We can start it in the morning before work, and come home to the long-cooked taste of Sunday dinner any night of the week.

Beef and Broccoli Stir-Fry

Serving Size: 1/6 recipe, Total Servings: 6

3/4 cup beef broth

1 tablespoon light soy sauce

1 teaspoon garlic powder

1/4 teaspoon ground ginger

1/2 teaspoon black pepper

1 tablespoon light brown sugar

1 tablespoon cornstarch

1 pound beef top or bottom round steak, cut into 1/4-inch julienne strips

2 medium onions, cut into 1/2-inch wedges

1 bunch broccoli, cut into florets

1. In a small bowl, combine the beef broth, soy sauce, garlic powder, ginger, pepper, brown sugar, and cornstarch; mix well and set aside.

2. Coat a large skillet or wok with nonstick cooking spray. Add the beef and brown over medium-high heat for 5 minutes, stirring frequently. Add the onions and broccoli, and cook for 3 to 4 minutes, or until the onion is tender.

3. Add the beef broth mixture to the skillet and stir constantly for 2 to 3 minutes, or until the sauce begins to thicken. Serve immediately.

Exchanges
2 Lean Meat
2 Vegetable

Calories	177
Calories from Fat	50
Total Fat	6 g
Saturated Fat	2 g
Cholesterol	44 mg
Sodium	344 mg
Carbohydrate	13 g
Dietary Fiber	4 g
Sugars	7 g
Protein	20 g

Did You Know...

that there are two simple secrets to successful stir-frying? They are cutting all the foods uniformly, and stirring them quickly over high heat. That's it! And in no time, your meat, poultry, or fish is ready, and your veggies are cooked-but-still-crunchy perfect!

Veal Loaf Florentine

Serving Size: 2 slices, Total Servings: 8

1-1/2 pounds ground veal

1 package (9 ounces) frozen
  creamed spinach, thawed

2 eggs

1 cup dry bread crumbs

1/2 teaspoon garlic powder

1 teaspoon salt

1/2 teaspoon pepper

1 Preheat the oven to 350°F.

2 In a large bowl, combine all the ingredients; mix well and form into a loaf on a large rimmed baking sheet.

3 Bake for 55 to 60 minutes, or until the meat is cooked through.

Exchanges
1 Starch
2 Lean Meat
1 Fat

Calories 236
  Calories from Fat 97
Total Fat ....11 g
  Saturated Fat ....4 g
Cholesterol ....128 mg
Sodium ....619 mg
Carbohydrate ....12 g
  Dietary Fiber ....1 g
  Sugars ....1 g
Protein ....21 g

Good for You!

We've always been told to "eat our spinach" because it's good for us. Well, here's a way to incorporate that goodness into our main dish. Take this to your next holiday potluck, and you're sure to be the hit of the party.

Seafood

Almond-Crusted Flounder

Serving Size: 1 fillet, Total Servings: 6

1 tablespoon sugar

3/4 teaspoon ground cinnamon

1/4 teaspoon ground red pepper

1/2 teaspoon salt

6 flounder fillets
(about 1-1/2 pounds total)

2 egg whites, beaten

1 cup sliced almonds (3 ounces)

2 tablespoons butter

2 tablespoons olive oil

1/2 cup amaretto liqueur

1 In a small bowl, combine the sugar, cinnamon, red pepper, and salt; mix well. Season the fillets with 1 teaspoon of the mixture, reserving the remaining mixture.

2 Place the egg whites in a shallow dish and the almonds in another shallow dish. Coat each fillet with the egg whites, then almonds.

3 In a large skillet, melt 1 tablespoon butter with 1 tablespoon olive oil over medium heat. Add 3 fillets and cook for 4 minutes, then turn and cook for 2 to 3 more minutes, or until the fish flakes easily with a fork; transfer to a serving platter and cover to keep warm. Repeat with the remaining fillets, adding the remaining butter and olive oil.

4 Add the reserved sugar mixture and the amaretto to the skillet; reduce the heat to low and cook for 1 to 2 minutes, or until thickened, stirring constantly. Pour over the fillets and serve immediately.

Exchanges
1 Carbohydrate
4 Lean Meat
1 Fat

Calories............................314
   Calories from Fat..........148
Total Fat..........................16 g
   Saturated Fat.....................3 g
Cholesterol.......................69 mg
Sodium............................348 mg
Carbohydrate...................17 g
   Dietary Fiber....................2 g
   Sugars...............................14 g
Protein.............................25 g

Did You Know...

that amaretto is an almond-flavored liqueur? That's why it's perfect in this almond-y dish.

Asian Fish

Serving Size: 1 fillet, Total Servings: 4

4 halibut fillets (4 ounces each)

2 tablespoons light soy sauce

1/3 cup dry sherry

1 tablespoon brown sugar

3/4 teaspoon ground ginger

1 package (6 ounces) frozen snow peas, thawed

1 can (15 ounces) whole baby corn, drained

1 Coat a large skillet with nonstick cooking spray and heat over medium-high heat until hot.

2 Add the fillets to the skillet and cook for 3 to 4 minutes per side, or until the fish flakes easily with a fork. Remove the fillets to a platter and cover to keep warm.

3 In a small bowl, combine the soy sauce, sherry, sugar, and ginger; add to the hot skillet. Cook over high heat for 2 minutes, or until the mixture begins to thicken, stirring constantly to loosen the particles on the bottom of the skillet.

4 Add the snow peas and corn, stirring until heated through. Return the fish to the skillet, turning to coat with the sauce.

5 Serve the fish topped with the vegetables and sauce.

Exchanges
1 Carbohydrate
4 Very Lean Meat

Calories............................204
   Calories from Fat.............24
Total Fat ....3 g
   Saturated Fat ....0 g
Cholesterol........................37 mg
Sodium ....379 mg
Carbohydrate...................14 g
   Dietary Fiber....................3 g
   Sugars..............................10 g
Protein ....26 g

Serving Tip

The next time your family craves Chinese food, try making this healthy option. And feel free to add any of your favorite veggies such as water chestnuts, bell peppers, or even bamboo shoots. They won't believe it's not take-out!

Mango Tango Fillets

Serving Size: 1 fillet with 1/2 cup salsa, Total Servings: 6

1 medium mango, peeled, pitted, and diced

1 red bell pepper, diced

1/2 of a small red onion, diced

1 can (8-1/4 ounces) pineapple tidbits, drained with juice reserved

1/4 teaspoon salt, divided

1/2 teaspoon ground red pepper, divided

6 white-fleshed fish fillets (2 pounds total) such as cod, orange roughy, or flounder

1 In a medium bowl, combine the mango, bell pepper, onion, pineapple, 1/8 teaspoon salt, and 1/4 teaspoon ground red pepper; mix well, cover, and chill.

2 Place the fish in a large skillet and pour the reserved pineapple juice over it. Sprinkle the fish with the remaining 1/8 teaspoon salt and 1/4 teaspoon ground red pepper.

3 Cover the fish and bring the liquid to a boil over high heat. Reduce the heat to low and cook for 7 to 8 minutes, or until the fish flakes easily with a fork. Serve immediately, topped with the chilled mango salsa.

Exchanges
4 Very Lean Meat
1 Fruit

Calories	183
Calories from Fat	9
Total Fat	1 g
Saturated Fat	0 g
Cholesterol	67 mg
Sodium	190 mg
Carbohydrate	15 g
Dietary Fiber	2 g
Sugars	12 g
Protein	28 g

Good for You!

The mango is an exotic fruit that is at its peak between May and September. So how about making this dish for a graduation dinner, "school's out" party, or whenever the mood strikes? Take advantage of mangoes, because, in addition to tasting good, they're chock-full of vitamins A and C!

Sesame-Crusted Swordfish

Serving Size: 1 fillet, Total Servings: 4

Juice of 2 lemons
(about 7 tablespoons)

1/4 cup vegetable oil

2 garlic cloves, minced

1/2 teaspoon salt

1/2 teaspoon black pepper

Four 1/2-inch-thick swordfish
steaks (about 1 pound total)

2 teaspoons sesame seeds

1 In a shallow dish, combine all the ingredients except the swordfish and sesame seeds; mix well. Add the swordfish and coat completely. Cover and marinate in the refrigerator for 2 hours, turning occasionally.

2 Coat a grill pan with nonstick cooking spray and heat over medium-high heat.

3 Remove the swordfish from the marinade; discard the marinade. Grill the fish for 4 to 5 minutes; turn the fish, sprinkle with sesame seeds, and grill for 4 to 5 more minutes, or until it flakes easily with a fork. Serve immediately.

Exchanges
3 Lean Meat
1 Fat

Calories	212
Calories from Fat	112
Total Fat	12 g
Saturated Fat	0 g
Cholesterol	43 mg
Sodium	251 mg
Carbohydrate	1 g
Dietary Fiber	0 g
Sugars	1 g
Protein	23 g

Preparation Tip
When buying fish, make sure it has a fresh odor and a firm, moist texture. Any type of fresh seafood should always be wrapped tightly, stored in the refrigerator, and preferably used within a day of purchase.

Sizzlin' Catfish

Serving Size: 1 fillet, Total Servings: 4

2 tablespoons vegetable oil

4 catfish fillets (1 pound total)

1/8 teaspoon salt

1/4 teaspoon black pepper

1 tablespoon lemon juice

1/4 pound fresh mushrooms, sliced

1 onion, chopped

1/4 cup chopped fresh parsley

1 In a large skillet, heat the oil over medium heat.

2 Season the catfish fillets with the salt and pepper. Add to the skillet and sprinkle with the lemon juice. Add the remaining ingredients to the skillet. Cook for 3 to 4 minutes per side, or until the fish flakes easily with a fork.

3 Serve the fish topped with the vegetables.

"Aside from the fact that it's really light, fish has so many nutrients that red meat lacks. So make sure to make fish part of your regular meal plan."

Exchanges
3 Lean Meat
1 Vegetable
1 Fat

Calories 241
 Calories from Fat 140
Total Fat ....16 g
 Saturated Fat ....2 g
Cholesterol ....65 mg
Sodium ....163 mg
Carbohydrate ....5 g
 Dietary Fiber ....1 g
 Sugars...............................3 g
Protein ....20 g

Florentine Fish Roll-Ups

Serving Size: 1 roll-up, Total Servings: 4

1 package (10 ounces) frozen chopped spinach, thawed and well drained

2 tablespoons grated Parmesan cheese

1/4 teaspoon garlic powder

1/4 teaspoon salt

1/4 teaspoon black pepper

4 white-fleshed fish fillets (about 6 ounces each), such as sole, flounder, or tilapia

Nonstick cooking spray

1/2 teaspoon paprika

1. Preheat the oven to 350°F. Coat a rimmed baking sheet with nonstick cooking spray.

2. In a medium bowl, combine the spinach, Parmesan cheese, garlic powder, salt, and pepper; mix well.

3. Spread the spinach mixture evenly over the fish fillets. Roll up jellyroll style and place seam side down on the baking sheet.

4. Lightly coat the fish with the cooking spray and sprinkle with the paprika. Bake for 18 to 22 minutes, or until the fish flakes easily with a fork.

"My grandkids made this for me (with a little help from their parents) on Grandparents Day, and now it's become a family favorite for many of our get-togethers. It's got that holiday look—but boy is it ever easy!"

Exchanges
5 Very Lean Meat
1 Vegetable

Calories	187
Calories from Fat	28
Total Fat	3 g
Saturated Fat	1 g
Cholesterol	93 mg
Sodium	398 mg
Carbohydrate	3 g
Dietary Fiber	2 g
Sugars	0 g
Protein	35 g

Greek Festival Fish

Serving Size: 1 fillet, Total Servings: 6

2 tablespoons olive oil

8 scallions, thinly sliced

2 cloves garlic, minced

4 tomatoes, chopped

1/2 cup dry white wine

2 tablespoons finely chopped
   parsley

1 teaspoon dried oregano

1 teaspoon black pepper

6 white-fleshed fish fillets
   (2 pounds total) such as
   tilapia, flounder, or sole

1 package (4 ounces) crumbled
   feta cheese

1 Preheat the oven to 400°F. Coat a
   9" × 13" baking dish with nonstick
   cooking spray.

2 In a medium skillet, heat the oil
   over medium heat. Add the
   scallions and garlic and sauté until
   tender. Add the tomatoes, wine,
   parsley, oregano, and pepper.
   Simmer for 5 minutes, or until the
   sauce thickens. Remove from the
   heat.

3 Place half of the sauce mixture in
   the baking dish. Arrange the fish
   fillets over the sauce and cover with
   the remaining sauce. Sprinkle with
   the feta cheese.

4 Bake for 15 to 18 minutes, or until
   the fish flakes easily with a fork.
   Serve immediately.

Exchanges
4 Lean Meat
1 Vegetable

Calories	259
Calories from Fat	91
Total Fat	10 g
Saturated Fat	4 g
Cholesterol	96 mg
Sodium	350 mg
Carbohydrate	8 g
Dietary Fiber	2 g
Sugars	5 g
Protein	32 g

Did You Know...
that you can cut down
on the saltiness of feta
cheese by soaking it in
fresh, cold water or
milk for a few
minutes?

Cod au Gratin

Serving Size: 1 fillet, Total Servings: 6

1 pound mushrooms, chopped

1 medium onion, chopped

1/2 cup fresh chopped parsley

1/2 teaspoon salt, divided

1/2 teaspoon black pepper, divided

6 cod fillets (about 2 pounds total)

3/4 cup dry white wine

3/4 cup plain bread crumbs

2 tablespoons butter, melted

1 cup (4 ounces) shredded Swiss cheese

1 Preheat the oven to 450°F. Coat a 9" × 13" baking dish with nonstick cooking spray.

2 In a medium bowl, combine the mushrooms, onion, parsley, 1/4 teaspoon salt, and 1/4 teaspoon pepper; mix well. Spoon into the baking dish. Place the cod fillets over the mushroom mixture and pour the wine over them.

3 In a medium bowl, combine the remaining ingredients, including the remaining 1/4 teaspoon salt and 1/4 teaspoon pepper; mix well. Sprinkle over the fish and bake for 15 to 20 minutes, or until the fish is golden and flakes easily with a fork. Serve immediately.

Exchanges
1 Carbohydrate
4 Lean Meat

Calories............................321
  Calories from Fat 99
Total Fat ....11 g
  Saturated Fat ....6 g
Cholesterol........................94 mg
Sodium ....496 mg
Carbohydrate...................16 g
  Dietary Fiber.....................2 g
  Sugars...............................3 g
Protein ....36 g

Change of Pace

Next Father's Day, instead of grilling, break with tradition and really give Dad the day off. Sit him down to this fancy-tasting fresh catch. And if Dad doesn't like Swiss cheese, that's no problem— substitute his favorite variety such as Cheddar, provolone, or Monterey Jack.

Mediterranean Baked Tuna

Serving Size: 1 tuna steak, Total Servings: 4

2 tablespoons olive oil, divided

Four 1/2-inch-thick tuna steaks
(about 1 pound total)

2 teaspoons balsamic vinegar

2 teaspoons dried rosemary

1/4 teaspoon crushed red pepper

1/4 teaspoon salt

2 medium plum tomatoes,
chopped

1 Preheat the oven to 350°F.

2 Sprinkle 1 tablespoon oil over the bottom of a 9" × 13" baking dish. Place the tuna in the baking dish and sprinkle with the remaining 1 tablespoon oil and the balsamic vinegar. Sprinkle the rosemary, red pepper, and salt evenly over the tuna.

3 Top the tuna with the tomatoes and bake for 12 to 15 minutes, or until the tuna is cooked to desired doneness.

Exchanges
4 Lean Meat

Calories...........................220
   Calories from Fat..........105
Total Fat...........................12 g
   Saturated Fat.....................1 g
Cholesterol.......................42 mg
Sodium..........................190 mg
Carbohydrate.....................2 g
   Dietary Fiber.....................1 g
   Sugars...............................1 g
Protein.............................26 g

Preparation Tip
This is a perfect dish to make if you like your tuna steak medium-rare or even rare. Just make sure to use very fresh tuna and reduce the cooking time to achieve the desired doneness.

Poached Salmon and Asparagus

Serving Size: 1 fillet, Total Servings: 4

4 salmon fillets (about 1 pound)

1 teaspoon dried rosemary

1/2 teaspoon black pepper, divided

1 can (14 ounces) ready-to-use vegetable broth

Juice of 1 lemon

1/2 pound fresh asparagus, trimmed and cut into 2-inch pieces

1 Season the salmon with the rosemary and 1/4 teaspoon pepper; place in a large skillet.

2 In a small bowl, combine the broth, lemon juice, and the remaining 1/4 teaspoon pepper; mix well and pour into the skillet. Cover and bring to a boil over medium heat. Reduce the heat to low and simmer for 5 minutes.

3 Add the asparagus around the salmon; cover, and cook for 5 more minutes, or until the fish flakes easily with a fork and the asparagus is tender. Serve immediately.

"I never throw out the liquid left over after poaching foods—and I hope you don't either. It can be used to make a sauce for the poached food, or as a soup base."

Exchanges
3 Lean Meat
1 Vegetable

Calories 209
  Calories from Fat 89
Total Fat .... 10 g
  Saturated Fat .... 0 g
Cholesterol .... 72 mg
Sodium .... 124 mg
Carbohydrate .... 3 g
  Dietary Fiber .... 1 g
  Sugars .... 1 g
Protein .... 25 g

Tempting Tuna Loaf

Serving Size: 2 slices, Total Servings: 6

1 can (12 ounces) chunk white tuna in water, drained and flaked

3/4 cup plain bread crumbs

1 small onion, finely chopped

2 eggs, beaten

1/4 cup low-fat (1%) milk

1/2 teaspoon lemon juice

1/2 teaspoon dried dill

1 tablespoon fresh chopped parsley

1/2 teaspoon salt

1/2 teaspoon black pepper

1 Preheat the oven to 350°F. Coat a 9" × 5" loaf pan with nonstick cooking spray.

2 In a large bowl, combine all the ingredients; mix well. Spread into the loaf pan.

3 Bake for 35 to 40 minutes, or until golden. Slice and serve.

"Move over meat loaf! Here's a fresh, light alternative that fits our meal plan to a 'T!'"

Exchanges
1 Starch
2 Very Lean Meat

Calories 149
  Calories from Fat 26
Total Fat ....3 g
  Saturated Fat ....1 g
Cholesterol ....86 mg
Sodium ....508 mg
Carbohydrate ....12 g
  Dietary Fiber ....1 g
  Sugars ....2 g
Protein ....17 g

Clams Pomodoro

Serving Size: 1/2 dozen clams, Total Servings: 4

2 dozen clams

1 can (14-1/2 ounces) stewed tomatoes, chopped with juice reserved

1/4 cup dry white wine

2 tablespoons chopped fresh basil

1/4 teaspoon black pepper

Lemon wedges for garnish, optional

1 In a large soup pot, combine all the ingredients, including the reserved stewed tomato juice.

2 Cover and bring to a boil over high heat; reduce the heat to low and simmer for 6 to 8 minutes, or until the clams open. Do not overcook. **Discard any clams that do not open.**

3 Remove to a serving bowl or individual bowls; serve garnished with lemon wedges, if desired.

Exchanges
3 Very Lean Meat
2 Vegetable

Calories	146
Calories from Fat	16
Total Fat	2 g
Saturated Fat	0 g
Cholesterol	50 mg
Sodium	347 mg
Carbohydrate	11 g
Dietary Fiber	1 g
Sugars	7 g
Protein	20 g

Did You Know...

that a clam should not be eaten if its shell is still tightly closed after cooking? The shell should open widely on its own during cooking. If it doesn't ... be safe and toss it!

See Photo Insert

Garlicky Scallop Stir-Fry

Serving Size: 1/8 recipe, Total Servings: 8

2 tablespoons butter

1/2 pound mushrooms, thinly sliced

2 garlic cloves, minced

1 can (10-1/2 ounces) condensed chicken broth

1 medium head broccoli, cut into small florets

1/2 of a small red bell pepper, diced

1-1/2 pounds sea scallops, quartered

3 tablespoons cornstarch

2 teaspoons light soy sauce

1 In a large skillet, melt the butter over high heat. Add the mushrooms and garlic and sauté for 2 to 3 minutes, or until the mushrooms are tender.

2 Reserve 1/4 cup chicken broth. Add the broccoli, bell pepper, and the remaining chicken broth to the skillet; mix well. Reduce the heat to medium and cook for 4 to 5 minutes, or until the broccoli is tender-crisp.

3 Add the scallops and cook for 1 to 2 minutes, or until the scallops are firm and white.

4 In a small bowl, combine the cornstarch, soy sauce, and the reserved chicken broth until smooth; stir into the skillet and cook for 1 minute, or until thickened. Serve immediately.

Exchanges
2 Very Lean Meat
1 Vegetable
1/2 Fat

Calories	113
Calories from Fat	36
Total Fat	4 g
Saturated Fat	2 g
Cholesterol	31 mg
Sodium	447 mg
Carbohydrate	7 g
Dietary Fiber	2 g
Sugars	2 g
Protein	12 g

"If there were an election for the best way to prepare scallops, this would be the hands-down winner! Maybe we should plan on serving this on Election Day as the results roll in ..."

Lemon-Lover's Scallops

Serving Size: About 6 scallops, Total Servings: 4

Nonstick cooking spray

1 large egg, beaten

1 tablespoon water

2 tablespoons lemon juice, divided

1/2 cup Italian-flavored bread crumbs

1-1/2 pounds sea scallops

1 Preheat the oven to 450°F. Coat a large rimmed baking sheet with nonstick cooking spray.

2 In a shallow dish, combine the egg, water, and 1 tablespoon lemon juice; mix well. Place the bread crumbs in another shallow dish.

3 Dip each scallop in the egg mixture, then in the bread crumbs, coating completely.

4 Place the scallops on the baking sheet; lightly coat the tops with nonstick cooking spray and drizzle with the remaining 1 tablespoon lemon juice. Bake for 15 to 20 minutes, or until golden, turning once during cooking.

Exchanges
1/2 Starch
4 Very Lean Meat

Calories............................172
   Calories from Fat.............29
Total Fat..............................3 g
   Saturated Fat......................1 g
Cholesterol.......................98 mg
Sodium............................461 mg
Carbohydrate...................11 g
   Dietary Fiber......................1 g
   Sugars...............................1 g
Protein.............................23 g

Finishing Touch

Dazzle 'em by drizzling some fresh-squeezed lemon, lime, or orange juice over the scallops just before serving.

Meatless Main Dishes

Greek Spinach Pie

Serving Size: 1 slice, Total Servings: 8

1 container (10 ounces) refrigerated pizza dough

1 small onion, chopped

1 garlic clove, minced

1/2 teaspoon dried basil

3/4 cup low-fat cottage cheese

1 package (4 ounces) crumbled feta cheese

3/4 cup evaporated skim milk

8 egg whites

2 packages (10 ounces each) frozen chopped spinach, thawed and squeezed dry

1 Preheat the oven to 350°F. Coat a 9-inch pie plate with nonstick cooking spray.

2 Unroll the pizza dough and form into a ball. On a lightly floured surface, slightly flatten the dough with your hands, then roll out the dough to form a 12-inch circle. Place in the pie plate to form a crust.

3 Lightly coat a medium skillet with nonstick cooking spray. Add the onion, garlic, and basil. Cook over medium heat for 3 to 4 minutes, or until the onion is tender, stirring constantly.

4 In a large bowl, beat together the cottage cheese and feta cheese until creamy and well mixed. Add the evaporated milk and egg whites and continue beating until well combined. Stir in the onion mixture and spinach.

5 Pour the mixture into the pie crust. Bake for 55 to 60 minutes, or until a knife inserted in the center comes out clean.

6 Let stand for 15 minutes, then cut into wedges and serve.

Exchanges
1-1/2 Carbohydrate
1 Lean Meat

Calories	191
Calories from Fat	39
Total Fat	4 g
Saturated Fat	2 g
Cholesterol	13 mg
Sodium	715 mg
Carbohydrate	24 g
Dietary Fiber	2 g
Sugars	7 g
Protein	15 g

"This one's a take-off on a traditional Greek favorite known as spanakopitta, which is simply spinach pie. We've captured the flavor and spirit of this Old World classic without all the old-time work. It's perfect for a Mother's Day brunch or any spring party!"

See Photo Insert

Veggie-Stuffed Burritos

Serving Size: 1 burrito, Total Servings: 5

1 teaspoon vegetable oil

2 onions, chopped

3 garlic cloves, minced

1 green bell pepper, chopped

1 zucchini, chopped

1 large carrot, grated

2 teaspoons chili powder

1 teaspoon dried oregano

1 teaspoon ground cumin

1-1/2 cups salsa, divided

1 can (16 ounces) vegetarian
   refried beans

Five 10-inch flour tortillas

1/2 cup (2 ounces) shredded
   Cheddar cheese

1 Preheat the oven to 400°F. Coat two 9" × 13" baking dishes with nonstick cooking spray.

2 In a large skillet, heat the oil over medium heat; add the onion and cook for 3 minutes, or until tender, stirring occasionally. Add the garlic, green pepper, zucchini, and carrot, and cook for 5 minutes, stirring often. Stir in the chili powder, oregano, and cumin.

3 Remove from the heat and stir in 3/4 cup salsa and the refried beans. Spoon equal amounts of the vegetable mixture over the centers of the tortillas.

4 Fold the bottom of each tortilla over the vegetable mixture, then fold both sides over envelope fashion. Fold over the top of each tortilla to close; place seam side down in the baking dish.

5 Pour the remaining 3/4 cup salsa evenly over the burritos. Bake for 15 minutes.

6 Sprinkle with the cheese and bake for 5 minutes, or until heated through and the cheese is melted. Serve immediately.

Exchanges
3-1/2 Starch
3 Vegetable
1-1/2 Fat

Calories..........................429
   Calories from Fat............95
Total Fat..........................11 g
   Saturated Fat....................4 g
Cholesterol......................12 mg
Sodium............................986 mg
Carbohydrate..................68 g
   Dietary Fiber..................11 g
   Sugars...............................11 g
Protein.............................16 g

Change of Pace

Stuffing burritos with yummy good-for-us veggies and vegetarian refried beans is the way to beat the "boring burrito blues!" Our Cinco de Mayo fiestas this May will be tastier than ever. Olé!

Eggplant Parmigiana

Serving Size: 3 slices, Total Servings: 6

1/2 cup plain dry bread crumbs

1 tablespoon grated Parmesan cheese

1 teaspoon dried oregano

1/4 cup all-purpose flour

2 eggs, lightly beaten

1 eggplant (12 to 15 ounces), trimmed and sliced crosswise into 1/4-inch slices

1 cup light spaghetti sauce

1/2 cup (2 ounces) finely shredded part-skim mozzarella cheese

Nonstick cooking spray

1. Preheat the oven to 350°F. Coat two 10" × 15" rimmed baking sheets with nonstick cooking spray.

2. Place the bread crumbs, Parmesan cheese, and oregano in a shallow dish; mix well. Place the flour in another shallow dish and place the eggs in a third shallow dish.

3. Dip the eggplant slices in the flour, then the eggs, then the bread crumb mixture, coating completely with each.

4. Arrange the eggplant in a single layer on the baking sheets. Lightly coat the tops of the eggplant with nonstick cooking spray. Bake for 25 to 30 minutes, or until golden.

5. Spoon the spaghetti sauce evenly over the eggplant slices, then sprinkle with the mozzarella cheese. Bake for 8 to 10 minutes, or until the cheese is melted. Serve immediately.

Exchanges
1 Carbohydrate
1 Fat

Calories	139
Calories from Fat	38
Total Fat	4 g
Saturated Fat	2 g
Cholesterol	78 mg
Sodium	372 mg
Carbohydrate	18 g
Dietary Fiber	3 g
Sugars	5 g
Protein	8 g

Good for You!

I'm betting that you've tried this classic dish at an Italian restaurant or two. Sure, it tastes rich and sinful. The usual gobs of cheese and the excess sauce may taste heavenly, but they can leave us bursting at the seams when we finish! I've smartened up! Now I prefer this version, 'cause it uses lighter ingredients that leave me feeling satisfied, not uncomfortably stuffed. I'm sure you'll feel the same.

Garden-Fresh Burgers

Serving Size: 1 patty, Total Servings: 6

3/4 cup dry bread crumbs, divided

1 tablespoon vegetable oil

1 medium onion, finely chopped

2 garlic cloves, minced

1 teaspoon dried thyme

3 cups warm cooked brown rice

1 medium carrot, peeled and grated

1/3 cup chopped fresh parsley

1/4 cup grated Parmesan cheese

3 tablespoons light soy sauce

2 eggs

1 Preheat the broiler. Coat a rimmed baking sheet with nonstick cooking spray. Place 1/2 cup bread crumbs in a shallow dish; set aside.

2 In a large nonstick skillet, heat the oil over medium-high heat. Sauté the onion, garlic, and thyme for 4 to 5 minutes, or until the onion is tender; transfer to a large bowl.

3 Add the remaining ingredients except the reserved bread crumbs; mix well.

4 Form the mixture into six 1/2-inch-thick patties and coat with the reserved 1/2 cup bread crumbs. Place on the baking sheet and broil for 6 to 7 minutes per side, or until golden and heated through.

Exchanges
2 Starch
1 Vegetable
1-1/2 Fat

Calories............................251
   Calories from Fat............65
Total Fat............................7 g
   Saturated Fat....................2 g
Cholesterol.......................76 mg
Sodium............................538 mg
Carbohydrate.................38 g
   Dietary Fiber....................3 g
   Sugars.............................5 g
Protein.............................9 g

Finishing Touch
Rain or shine, broiled or grilled, whatever the occasion, these year-round garden-fresh favorites taste even better dipped in warm spaghetti sauce.

Falafel Patties

Serving Size: 3 patties, Total Servings: 8

2 cans (15 ounces each) chick peas (garbanzo beans), drained and rinsed

1/2 cup plain dry bread crumbs

1/2 cup fresh chopped parsley

1 small onion, minced

2 garlic cloves, minced

1 egg

1 teaspoon fresh lemon juice

2 tablespoons water

1 teaspoon ground cumin

1/8 teaspoon ground red pepper

1/4 teaspoon salt

1/4 teaspoon black pepper

1 In a food processor fitted with its metal cutting blade, process all the ingredients until thoroughly combined. Cover and chill for 30 minutes.

2 Shape the mixture into 24 patties, about 2 inches wide and 1/2 inch thick.

3 Coat a large skillet with nonstick cooking spray. Heat the skillet over medium heat. Add the patties in batches and cook for 3 minutes per side, or until crispy and golden. Serve warm.

Exchanges
2 Starch

Calories............................163
    Calories from Fat............27
Total Fat ....3 g
    Saturated Fat ....0 g
Cholesterol.........................27 mg
Sodium ....247 mg
Carbohydrate.....................27 g
    Dietary Fiber......................6 g
    Sugars..............................5 g
Protein ....8 g

Finishing Touch

I like to serve this Middle Eastern favorite in whole wheat pita bread with shredded lettuce, chopped tomatoes, and cucumber, and finish it off with a small dollop of tahini— a smooth sesame seed paste.

Greenhouse Stuffed Peppers

Serving Size: 1/2 pepper, Total Servings: 4

2 bell peppers (any color), split lengthwise and cleaned

2 tablespoons olive oil

1 onion, chopped

4 garlic cloves, minced

2 ripe tomatoes, finely chopped

1/4 teaspoon salt

1/4 cup chopped fresh parsley

1/3 cup plain dry bread crumbs

2 tablespoons dry white wine

1/4 teaspoon black pepper

Grated Parmesan cheese for sprinkling (optional)

1 Preheat the oven to 350°F. Coat an 8-inch square baking dish with nonstick cooking spray.

2 Fill a medium saucepan half full with water and bring to a boil. Carefully place the pepper halves in the boiling water and boil for 4 to 5 minutes, or just until they begin to soften. Remove the peppers from the boiling water and plunge into cold water; drain and set aside.

3 In a large skillet, heat the olive oil over medium heat. Add the onion and garlic and sauté just until softened; do not burn. Remove from the heat and add the remaining ingredients except the pepper halves and the Parmesan cheese; mix well.

4 Fill the pepper halves with equal amounts of the mixture and place in the baking dish. Sprinkle with the Parmesan cheese, if desired. Bake for 35 to 40 minutes, until the filling is heated through.

Exchanges

1-1/2 Carbohydrate
1 Fat

Calories	156
Calories from Fat	65
Total Fat	7 g
Saturated Fat	1 g
Cholesterol	0 mg
Sodium	237 mg
Carbohydrate	21 g
Dietary Fiber	4 g
Sugars	9 g
Protein	3 g

Serving Tip

Get into the spirit of Earth Day! Enjoy the bounty of fresh veggies from your garden! These veggie-stuffed peppers look and taste great served over a pool of warm marinara sauce and topped with a sprinkle of Parmesan cheese.

Zucchini Corn Bread Pie

Serving Size: 1 wedge, Total Servings: 8

2 medium zucchini, quartered and thinly sliced

1 small onion, chopped

1/2 cup evaporated skim milk

2 eggs

1 package (8.5 ounces) corn muffin mix

1/2 cup finely shredded reduced-fat sharp Cheddar cheese, divided

1 Preheat the oven to 375°F. Coat a 9-inch pie plate with nonstick cooking spray. Coat a skillet with nonstick cooking spray.

2 Heat the skillet to medium heat. Sauté the zucchini and onion for 3 to 4 minutes, or until the zucchini is crisp-tender; set aside.

3 In a large bowl, beat together the evaporated milk and eggs. Stir in the corn muffin mix just until combined. Add the zucchini mixture and 1/4 cup cheese; mix well, then pour into the pie plate and sprinkle with the remaining 1/4 cup cheese.

4 Bake for 25 to 30 minutes, or until golden and a wooden toothpick inserted in the center comes out clean. Cut into wedges and serve.

Exchanges
1-1/2 Starch
1 Fat

Calories............................154
   Calories from Fat.............52
Total Fat.............................6 g
   Saturated Fat.....................3 g
Cholesterol.......................61 mg
Sodium............................321 mg
Carbohydrate...................26 g
   Dietary Fiber.....................2 g
   Sugars................................9 g
Protein..............................7 g

Serving Tip

Protein, carbs, and veggies ... this meal has it all! And don't be afraid to substitute other vegetables. It can still be "easy as pie!"

Asparagus Risotto

Serving Size: 1 cup, Total Servings: 4

2 tablespoons butter

2 tablespoons olive oil

1 small onion, finely chopped

1 cup long- or whole-grain rice

1 can (14 ounces) reduced-
    sodium chicken broth

1 can (15 ounces) asparagus
    cuts, drained and mashed

1/2 cup grated Parmesan cheese

1 In a medium saucepan, heat the butter and oil over medium-high heat. Add the onion and cook for 4 to 5 minutes, or until golden.

2 Add the rice and cook for 1 minute, stirring until the rice is coated. Add the broth and bring to a boil. Reduce the heat to low, cover, and simmer for 15 minutes.

3 Add the asparagus, cover, and cook for 5 minutes.

4 Add the Parmesan cheese and stir until the liquid is absorbed and the rice is creamy. Serve immediately.

Exchanges
3 Starch
2 Fat

Calories 312
    Calories from Fat 118
Total Fat ....13 g
    Saturated Fat ....5 g
Cholesterol ....17 mg
Sodium ....500 mg
Carbohydrate ....41 g
    Dietary Fiber....................2 g
    Sugars............................3 g
Protein ....7 g

Did You Know...

that risotto is the name for a traditional Italian rice dish and refers more to a cooking method than to particular flavorings? Risotto is known for being smooth and creamy, and can team any variety of ingredients with almost any kind of rice, although Arborio is the type traditionally used.

Stuffed Zucchini Boats

Serving Size: 2 zucchini halves plus filling, Total Servings: 4

4 medium zucchini

2 tablespoons olive oil

1 small onion, chopped

3 garlic cloves, minced

1/2 cup grated Swiss cheese

2 tablespoons all-purpose flour

2 tablespoons chopped fresh
   parsley

2 eggs, beaten

1/4 teaspoon salt

1/8 teaspoon black pepper

2 tablespoons grated Parmesan
   cheese

1 Preheat the oven to 375°F. Cut the zucchini lengthwise and scoop out the centers, leaving the shells 1/2 inch thick. Finely chop the meat from the center of the zucchini.

2 In a large skillet, heat the oil over medium-high heat and sauté the chopped zucchini, onion, and garlic for 3 to 5 minutes, or until the onion is tender.

3 In a large bowl, combine the Swiss cheese, flour, parsley, eggs, salt, and pepper; mix well. Stir in the vegetable mixture.

4 Fill the zucchini shells with the mixture and sprinkle the tops with the Parmesan cheese. Bake for 30 to 35 minutes, or until the filling is firm and golden.

Exchanges
1 Medium-Fat Meat
2 Vegetable
2 Fat

Calories...........................211
   Calories from Fat..........123
Total Fat ....14 g
   Saturated Fat ....6 g
Cholesterol......................123 mg
Sodium ....285 mg
Carbohydrate..................13 g
   Dietary Fiber.....................3 g
   Sugars...............................6 g
Protein ....11 g

Did You Know...

that zucchini wasn't introduced to America until the 1920s? Since zucchini means "small squash" in Italian, why not commemorate the arrival of our very first Italian "import," Christopher Columbus, by making these mouthwatering veggie boats?

Spicy Baked Linguine

Serving Size: 1/8 recipe, Total Servings: 8

1 pound linguine

1 tablespoon vegetable oil

1 medium zucchini, cut into
   1-inch chunks

1 large red bell pepper, cut into
   1-inch chunks

1 medium eggplant, cut into
   1-inch chunks

1 jar (26 ounces) light spaghetti
   sauce

1 cup salsa

3/4 cup (3 ounces) shredded
   reduced-fat mozzarella cheese

1 Preheat the oven to 350°F. Coat a 9" × 13" baking dish with nonstick cooking spray. Cook the linguine according to the package directions; drain, rinse, drain again, and set aside.

2 Meanwhile, heat the oil in a soup pot over medium-high heat; add the zucchini, pepper, and eggplant. Sauté for 6 to 8 minutes, or until tender.

3 Stir in the spaghetti sauce and salsa, then add the linguine and mix well. Place the linguine mixture in the baking dish.

4 Top with the cheese and bake for 25 to 30 minutes, or until the linguine is heated through and the cheese is melted.

Exchanges
3 Starch
3 Vegetable
1/2 Fat

Calories............................319
   Calories from Fat............40
Total Fat............................4 g
   Saturated Fat....................1 g
Cholesterol..........................6 mg
Sodium............................614 mg
Carbohydrate..................58 g
   Dietary Fiber....................7 g
   Sugars..............................12 g
Protein..............................13 g

"I love to serve this meal just before the holidays, when family is around and the weather is getting chilly. It's a sure crowd-pleaser that goes together in no time."

Penne Toss

Serving Size: 1/8 recipe, Total Servings: 8

1 pound penne pasta

1 can (28 ounces) diced
   tomatoes, undrained

1/4 cup olive oil

1 small onion, chopped

3 garlic cloves, minced

1 tablespoon red wine vinegar

1/2 teaspoon dried oregano

1/4 teaspoon salt

1/2 teaspoon black pepper

1 cup (4 ounces) shredded
   mozzarella cheese

1/4 cup chopped fresh basil

1 Cook the pasta according to the package directions; drain.

2 Meanwhile, in a large bowl, combine the diced tomatoes, olive oil, onion, garlic, vinegar, oregano, salt, and pepper; mix well. Add the cooked pasta; toss to coat.

3 Sprinkle with the mozzarella cheese and chopped basil, and toss again; serve warm.

Exchanges
3 Starch
2 Fat

Calories	328
Calories from Fat	86
Total Fat	10 g
Saturated Fat	3 g
Cholesterol	8 mg
Sodium	340 mg
Carbohydrate	47 g
Dietary Fiber	3 g
Sugars	6 g
Protein	14 g

Change of Pace

On Labor Day, a day when we all shouldn't have to "labor," this makes the perfect alternative to the "same old, same old" pasta salad. It's quick to throw together, and the tomatoes and basil help us linger over the fresh tastes of summer.

Bow Ties 'n' Veggies

Serving Size: 1/6 recipe, Total Servings: 6

1 package (8 ounces) bow tie pasta

2 tablespoons olive oil

1/2 of a medium-sized red onion, chopped

1/2 pound fresh asparagus spears, trimmed and cut into 1-inch pieces

1/2 pound fresh mushrooms, sliced

2 garlic cloves, minced

1/4 cup dry white wine

1 package (3 ounces) sun-dried tomatoes, reconstituted and sliced

1/2 teaspoon salt

1/2 teaspoon black pepper

1/2 cup half-and-half

1 package (10 ounces) fresh baby spinach, cut into 1/2-inch strips

1 tablespoon chopped fresh basil

1. Cook the pasta according to the package directions; drain and place in a large bowl.

2. Meanwhile, in a large skillet, heat the oil over medium-high heat. Add the onion and asparagus and sauté for 3 minutes. Add the mushrooms and garlic and sauté for 2 more minutes.

3. Stir in the wine, sun-dried tomatoes, salt, and pepper, and cook for 2 to 3 minutes. Add the half-and-half and cook until heated through.

4. Toss the sauce, spinach, and basil into the pasta until well combined. Serve immediately.

Exchanges

2 Starch	1-1/2 Fat
2 Vegetable	

Calories 272
   Calories from Fat 71
Total Fat .... 8 g
   Saturated Fat .... 2 g
Cholesterol .... 7 mg
Sodium .... 248 mg
Carbohydrate .... 42 g
   Dietary Fiber .... 5 g
   Sugars .... 9 g
Protein .... 10 g

"Our bountiful summer veggies are not only good for us, but they go a long way in stretching our dishes. Enjoy your favorite pasta with this rainbow of hearty helpers, and I promise your next picnic will be oh-so-colorful!"

Side Dishes

Baked Stuffed Spuds

Serving Size: 1 potato half, Total Servings: 6

3 medium baking potatoes, scrubbed and pierced with a fork

1 package (10 ounces) frozen spinach, thawed and drained

1/2 cup reduced-fat sour cream

1 tablespoon butter

1/2 teaspoon onion powder

1/2 teaspoon salt

1/2 teaspoon black pepper

Paprika for sprinkling

1 Preheat the oven to 400°F. Place the potatoes on a rimmed baking sheet and bake for 1 to 1-1/4 hours, or until fork-tender.

2 Cut the potatoes in half lengthwise and scoop out the pulp, placing it in a medium bowl.

3 Add the spinach, sour cream, butter, onion powder, salt, and pepper; with an electric beater on medium speed, mix until smooth and creamy. Spoon the mixture back into the potato shells and place on the baking sheet.

4 Sprinkle lightly with paprika and bake for 20 to 30 minutes, or until the tops begin to brown.

Exchanges

2 Starch

Calories	152
Calories from Fat	34
Total Fat	4 g
Saturated Fat	2 g
Cholesterol	12 mg
Sodium	265 mg
Carbohydrate	27 g
Dietary Fiber	3 g
Sugars	2 g
Protein	5 g

"Yup, most diabetes meal plans can incorporate baked stuffed potatoes—as long as we're moderate with the fillings and keep it to just one serving."

Garlic Roasted Potatoes

Serving Size: 1/6 recipe, Total Servings: 6

2 pounds small red potatoes, washed and quartered

12 garlic cloves, cut in half

2 tablespoons olive oil

1/4 teaspoon salt

1/4 teaspoon black pepper

1 Preheat the oven to 425°F. Coat a rimmed baking sheet with nonstick cooking spray.

2 In a medium bowl, combine all the ingredients and toss to evenly coat the potatoes.

3 Place the potatoes on the baking sheet and bake for 50 to 60 minutes, or until fork-tender. Serve immediately.

Exchanges
2 Starch
1/2 Fat

Calories	178
Calories from Fat	38
Total Fat	4 g
Saturated Fat	1 g
Cholesterol	0 mg
Sodium	108 mg
Carbohydrate	33 g
Dietary Fiber	3 g
Sugars	4 g
Protein	3 g

Did You Know...

that in addition to its intense flavor, garlic has been shown to be good for us? That's right! Eating garlic can lower blood glucose and cholesterol levels as well as boost the immune system, thwart viruses, and fight fatigue. With that kind of a reputation, garlic is worth the lingering aroma, so dig in ... and be sure to keep a breath mint on hand for later.

Beet Mashed Potatoes

Serving Size: 1/2 cup, Total Servings: 8

6 medium potatoes
   (about 2 pounds), peeled
   and cut into chunks

1 can (15 ounces) beets,
   undrained

1/4 cup (1/2 stick) butter,
   softened

1/4 teaspoon onion powder

1/2 teaspoon salt

1/2 teaspoon black pepper

1 Place the potatoes in a soup pot and add just enough water to cover them. Add the beets and their liquid and bring to a boil over high heat. Reduce the heat to medium and cook for 12 to 15 minutes, or until the potatoes are fork-tender; drain and place in a large bowl.

2 Add the remaining ingredients to the potatoes, and beat with an electric beater on medium speed until well blended. Serve immediately.

Exchanges
1-1/2 Starch
1/2 Fat

Calories............................138
   Calories from Fat............53
Total Fat ....6 g
   Saturated Fat ....4 g
Cholesterol........................15 mg
Sodium ....281 mg
Carbohydrate...................20 g
   Dietary Fiber.....................2 g
   Sugars...............................3 g
Protein ....2 g

Preparation Tip

Why not serve this on Earth Day, April 22, as a salute to the delicious earthy-red root? Or substitute a thawed and drained 10-ounce package of frozen chopped spinach for the beets and make it part of your St. Patrick's Day celebration!

See Photo Insert

Checkerboard Spuds & Squash

Serving Size: 3/4 cup, Total Servings: 9

4 cups warm mashed potatoes

2 tablespoons butter, melted and divided

2 scallions, chopped

1/4 teaspoon black pepper

3 packages (12 ounces each) frozen butternut squash, thawed and drained

1 tablespoon maple syrup

1/4 teaspoon ground cinnamon

1/8 teaspoon salt

1 Preheat the oven to 350°F. Coat an 8-inch square baking dish with nonstick cooking spray.

2 In a medium bowl, combine the mashed potatoes, melted butter, scallions, and black pepper; mix well and set aside.

3 In another medium bowl, combine the squash, maple syrup, cinnamon, and salt; mix well.

4 Spoon five equal-sized scoops of the potato mixture into the baking dish, placing one scoop in each corner and one scoop in the center. Using a spoon, shape each scoop into a square.

5 Place the squash mixture into the four empty squares, dividing it equally. Pat down evenly to fill any gaps, forming a checkerboard pattern. Bake for 45 to 50 minutes, or until heated through.

Exchanges
1-1/2 Starch
1/2 Fat

Calories............................133
    Calories from Fat.............29
Total Fat.............................3 g
    Saturated Fat......................2 g
Cholesterol...........................7 mg
Sodium.............................141 mg
Carbohydrate...................26 g
    Dietary Fiber......................4 g
    Sugars...............................5 g
Protein ....3 g

"Do you know the saying, 'We eat with our eyes?' Well, this showstopper is one classy dish! Whatever the occasion, your guests will love this eye-pleasin' go-along."

Nutty Brown Rice

Serving Size: 1/2 cup, Total Servings: 10

1 tablespoon vegetable oil

1 small onion, chopped

1 can (10-1/2 ounces)
   condensed chicken broth

3/4 cup water

1 cup uncooked brown rice
   (not instant rice)

1 teaspoon ground cumin

1/2 teaspoon black pepper

1 can (16 ounces) Great
   Northern beans, rinsed
   and drained

4 plum tomatoes, seeded,
   chopped, and drained

1 In a large skillet, heat the oil over medium heat; add the onion and sauté for 2 to 3 minutes, or until tender.

2 Add the broth, water, rice, cumin, and pepper; mix well. Bring to a boil, then reduce the heat to low.

3 Cover and simmer for 30 minutes, or until all the liquid is absorbed.

4 With a spoon, gently stir in the beans and tomatoes; cook for 5 minutes, or until heated through.

Exchanges
1-1/2 Starch
1/2 Fat

Calories............................142
   Calories from Fat............23
Total Fat.................................3 g
   Saturated Fat.....................0 g
Cholesterol..........................1 mg
Sodium............................264 mg
Carbohydrate...................25 g
   Dietary Fiber.....................3 g
   Sugars...............................3 g
Protein................................5 g

Good for You!

It's okay to indulge in this flavor-packed side dish. Because it has its bran intact, brown rice is high in fiber, giving it the edge on goodness.

Festive Pilaf

Serving Size: 1/2 cup, Total Servings: 8

1 tablespoon butter

1 cup uncooked long- or
   whole-grain rice, divided

2 chicken bouillon cubes

2 cups water

3 scallions, sliced

1/2 of a medium-sized red bell
   pepper, finely chopped

1/8 teaspoon black pepper

1 In a large skillet, melt the butter over high heat. Brown 1/2 cup rice in the butter, stirring constantly.

2 Add the remaining 1/2 cup rice, the bouillon cubes, and water, and bring to a boil. Reduce the heat to medium-low, cover, and simmer for 18 to 20 minutes.

3 Stir in the scallions, and the red and black pepper, and cook until heated through.

Exchanges
1 Starch
1/2 Fat

Calories	103
Calories from Fat	14
Total Fat	2 g
Saturated Fat	1 g
Cholesterol	4 mg
Sodium	242 mg
Carbohydrate	20 g
Dietary Fiber	1 g
Sugars	1 g
Protein	2 g

Finishing Touch
Top off this tasty go-along with a few scallion rings for an even more festive look!

Golden Polenta

Serving Size: 1 slice, Total Servings: 12

4 cups water

1/4 cup (1/2 stick) butter

1 teaspoon salt

2 cups fine-ground yellow cornmeal

1 Coat a 9" × 5" loaf pan with non-stick cooking spray.

2 In a large saucepan, combine the water, butter, and salt over high heat and bring to a boil. Remove from the heat and slowly whisk in the cornmeal until the mixture is smooth and no lumps remain.

3 Spoon the mixture into the loaf pan, packing it down firmly.

4 Allow to cool for at least 1 hour, or until firm. Invert the pan over a cutting board to remove the polenta. Slice, and serve.

Exchanges
1 Starch
1 Fat

Calories............................119
   Calories from Fat............38
Total Fat................................4 g
   Saturated Fat....................2 g
Cholesterol........................10 mg
Sodium.............................234 mg
Carbohydrate...................18 g
   Dietary Fiber.....................2 g
   Sugars..............................0 g
Protein...............................2 g

Serving Tip

This versatile Northern Italian staple fits every season. It's at home on the grill in summer with a juicy steak, perfect pan-fried in spring and fall—maybe teamed with fried chicken—and sure is comforting accompanying our wintry roasts and their flavorful pan juices. Mmm mmm!

Lemon–Basil Couscous

Serving Size: 3/4 cup, Total Servings: 10

1 package (10 ounces) couscous

1 can (15 ounces) garbanzo beans (chick peas), rinsed and drained

1/4 cup chopped fresh basil

1/2 of a medium-sized red onion, chopped

1 medium-sized tomato, chopped

Juice of 2 lemons (about 7 tablespoons)

1/4 teaspoon black pepper

1 Prepare the couscous according to the package directions; place in a large bowl and allow to cool.

2 Add the remaining ingredients; toss until well combined.

3 Cover and chill for at least 1 hour before serving.

Exchanges
2 Starch

Calories	163
Calories from Fat	19
Total Fat	2 g
Saturated Fat	0 g
Cholesterol	0 mg
Sodium	50 mg
Carbohydrate	30 g
Dietary Fiber	4 g
Sugars	3 g
Protein	6 g

Did You Know...

that couscous is a tiny bead-shaped grain product made from semolina? A staple in North African cultures, couscous is popular in many cultures today, and its flavorings vary from country to country. There are sweet versions, others, like the Moroccan version, that traditionally include saffron, and still others that are spiced up with hot pepper sauces. With so many variations, couscous is an ideal side dish that cooks up quickly and fits almost any main course.

Broccoli and Corn Casserole

Serving Size: 1/2 cup, Total Servings: 6

3/4 cup coarsely crumbled saltine crackers, divided

3 tablespoons butter, melted

1 package (10 ounces) frozen chopped broccoli, thawed and drained

1 can (16 ounces) cream-style corn

1 egg, beaten

1/3 cup grated Parmesan cheese

1/2 teaspoon onion powder

1/2 teaspoon black pepper

1 Preheat the oven to 350°F. Coat a 9" × 5" loaf pan with nonstick cooking spray.

2 In a large bowl, combine the cracker crumbs and melted butter; mix well. Reserve 1/3 cup of the cracker crumb mixture and set aside. Add the remaining ingredients to the large bowl; mix well and spoon into the loaf pan.

3 Sprinkle the top with the reserved cracker crumb mixture and bake for 40 to 45 minutes, or until heated through and the top is golden.

Exchanges
1 Starch
1 Vegetable
2 Fat

Calories	196
Calories from Fat	90
Total Fat	10 g
Saturated Fat	5 g
Cholesterol	57 mg
Sodium	525 mg
Carbohydrate	21 g
Dietary Fiber	3 g
Sugars	5 g
Protein	7 g

"This can be a side or main dish … it is up to you. Everything's in one pan—your protein, carbohydrates, and vegetables—so it's perfect! Now remember: Corn is classified as a carbohydrate, not a vegetable."

Autumn Squash

Serving Size: 3/4 cup, Total Servings: 8

2 medium zucchini, sliced

2 yellow squash, sliced

2 medium onions, sliced

2 tomatoes, quartered

2 garlic cloves, minced

2 tablespoons olive oil

1/2 cup pitted green or black
  olives

1/2 teaspoon salt

1/4 teaspoon black pepper

1 In a large skillet or wok, combine all the ingredients.

2 Cook over medium heat for about 20 minutes, or until the zucchini and yellow squash are tender, stirring occasionally.

Exchanges
2 Vegetable
1 Fat

Calories	82
Calories from Fat	41
Total Fat	5 g
Saturated Fat	1 g
Cholesterol	0 mg
Sodium	342 mg
Carbohydrate	9 g
Dietary Fiber	3 g
Sugars	5 g
Protein	2 g

Finishing Touch

Serve this on a platter with your famous pot roast or whatever main attraction you have planned.

Garden Veggie Muffins

Serving Size: 1 muffin, Total Servings: 6

1 onion, finely chopped

2 carrots, grated

1/2 of a green bell pepper, finely chopped

1 zucchini, shredded

1/3 cup shredded Swiss cheese

1-1/4 cups dry bread crumbs

1/2 teaspoon dried dill

1/4 teaspoon salt

1/4 teaspoon black pepper

1/2 cup light mayonnaise

2 eggs

1 Preheat the oven to 350°F. Coat a 6-cup muffin pan with nonstick cooking spray.

2 In a large bowl, combine the onion, carrots, green pepper, zucchini, cheese, bread crumbs, dill, salt, and black pepper.

3 In a small bowl, beat the mayonnaise and eggs until smooth; stir into the vegetable mixture until well combined.

4 Distribute the batter evenly among the muffin cups, and bake for 40 to 45 minutes, or until lightly browned.

Exchanges
1 Starch
2 Vegetable
2 Fat

Calories 231
   Calories from Fat 103
Total Fat ....11 g
   Saturated Fat ....3 g
Cholesterol ....83 mg
Sodium ....496 mg
Carbohydrate ....24 g
   Dietary Fiber ....2 g
   Sugars ....5 g
Protein ....8 g

"Working veggies into your meal plan is easy, especially when you get the double bonus of easy portion control that you get with muffins! A basket of these on your Mother's Day brunch buffet is sure to make Mom smile!"

Easy Carrot Bake

Serving Size: 1 square, Total Servings: 12

3 jars (4 ounces each) carrot
   baby food

1/2 cup (1 stick) butter, melted

3 eggs

1 cup all-purpose flour

1 cup packed light brown sugar

1 tablespoon lemon juice

1 teaspoon vanilla extract

1 teaspoon baking soda

1 teaspoon baking powder

1 Preheat the oven to 350°F. Coat an 8-inch square baking dish with nonstick cooking spray.

2 In a large bowl, combine the carrots and butter; mix well. Add the remaining ingredients; mix until well blended, then pour into the baking dish.

3 Bake for 35 to 40 minutes, or until a wooden toothpick inserted in the center comes out clean.

Exchanges
2 Carbohydrate
1-1/2 Fat

Calories	204
Calories from Fat	81
Total Fat	9 g
Saturated Fat	5 g
Cholesterol	73 mg
Sodium	257 mg
Carbohydrate	28 g
Dietary Fiber	1 g
Sugars	19 g
Protein	3 g

Great Go-Along

Talk about "no-fuss" … this satisfying go-along requires no mashing, no chopping, no worries! Our baby food shortcut is the answer. It's like having an extra pair of hands in the kitchen!

Mexican Corn Bread

Serving Size: 1 square, Total Servings: 9

1-1/2 cups self-rising cornmeal

1 can (8-3/4 ounces) cream-style corn

3 scallions, thinly sliced

1/4 cup chopped red bell pepper

3/4 cup shredded Mexican cheese blend, divided

1 cup reduced-fat sour cream

1/2 cup vegetable oil

2 eggs

1 Preheat the oven to 350°F. Coat an 8-inch square baking dish with nonstick cooking spray.

2 In a large bowl, combine all the ingredients except 1/4 cup cheese; mix well, then pour into the baking dish and sprinkle with the reserved 1/4 cup cheese.

3 Bake for 50 to 55 minutes, or until a wooden toothpick inserted in the center comes out clean. Cut into squares and serve warm.

"This is a welcome change from the normal side serving of bread, so go ahead and spice things up a little. You won't regret it!"

See Photo Insert

Exchanges
1-1/2 Starch
4 Fat

Calories	298
Calories from Fat	174
Total Fat	19 g
Saturated Fat	4 g
Cholesterol	65 mg
Sodium	491 mg
Carbohydrate	24 g
Dietary Fiber	2 g
Sugars	4 g
Protein	8 g

Stuffed Artichokes

Serving Size: 1 artichoke, Total Servings: 4

4 large artichokes, trimmed

2 tablespoons olive oil, divided

2 tablespoons butter

1 medium onion, chopped

1/4 pound fresh mushrooms, chopped

2 teaspoons minced garlic

1/2 cup Italian-flavored bread crumbs

2 teaspoons grated Parmesan cheese

1 Preheat the oven to 375°F. Place the artichokes in a large pot and fill the pot with just enough water to cover them. Bring to a boil over high heat and cook for 35 to 40 minutes, or until the artichokes are tender. Remove the artichokes and drain upside down; place right side up in an 8-inch square baking dish and set aside.

2 In a medium skillet, heat 1 table-spoon olive oil and the butter over medium heat; add the onion, mush-rooms, and garlic, and cook for 3 to 5 minutes, or until the vegetables are tender. Remove from the heat and stir in the bread crumbs and Parmesan cheese.

3 Scoop out the center of each arti-choke, making "pockets." Divide the stuffing mixture equally among the 4 artichokes.

4 Drizzle the remaining 1 tablespoon olive oil over the artichokes. Cover with aluminum foil and bake for 15 to 20 minutes, or until hot. Serve immediately.

Exchanges
2 Carbohydrate
2 Fat

Calories...........................248
   Calories from Fat..........125
Total Fat..........................14 g
   Saturated Fat.....................5 g
Cholesterol.......................16 mg
Sodium...........................412 mg
Carbohydrate..................30 g
   Dietary Fiber.....................3 g
   Sugars..............................5 g
Protein...........................9 g

Did You Know...
that, besides being an easy and tasty way to fancy up a party, artichokes are a super source of vitamin C, low in sodium, and fat-free?!

Roasted Plum Tomatoes

Serving Size: 4 tomato halves, Total Servings: 6

2 tablespoons vegetable oil

1 teaspoon salt

1/4 teaspoon black pepper

1/4 teaspoon garlic powder

1/4 teaspoon onion powder

12 plum tomatoes

2 tablespoons chopped fresh basil

1 Preheat the oven to 450°F. In a large bowl, combine all the ingredients except the tomatoes and basil.

2 Cut the tomatoes in half lengthwise and gently squeeze out the seeds and juice. Toss in the oil mixture then pour into a 9" × 13" baking dish.

3 Roast for 20 to 25 minutes, or until tender but not overcooked. Sprinkle with the basil, and serve.

Exchanges
1 Vegetable
1 Fat

Calories	68
Calories from Fat	46
Total Fat	5 g
Saturated Fat	0 g
Cholesterol	0 mg
Sodium	398 mg
Carbohydrate	6 g
Dietary Fiber	1 g
Sugars	3 g
Protein	1 g

Change of Pace

Try a side of flavorful, juicy plum tomatoes to add excitement to tonight's dinner. If you serve them simply roasted this way, your gang will surely be checking their calendars to see what the special occasion is!

See Photo Insert

Simply Spinach

Serving Size: 1 cup, Total Servings: 4

1 package (10 ounces) fresh
   spinach, cleaned and trimmed

1/2 teaspoon garlic powder

2 tablespoons olive oil

1/4 teaspoon salt

1/8 teaspoon black pepper

1 In a large pot, toss the spinach with the remaining ingredients.

2 Cook over medium heat for 4 to 5 minutes, or until the spinach leaves are wilted, stirring often. Serve immediately.

Exchanges
1 Vegetable
1 Fat

Calories	72
Calories from Fat	57
Total Fat	6 g
Saturated Fat	1 g
Cholesterol	0 mg
Sodium	202 mg
Carbohydrate	3 g
Dietary Fiber	2 g
Sugars	0 g
Protein	2 g

Preparation Tip
Most of the packaged spinach we buy today is pre-washed and ready to eat and cook, which sure saves us time. However, if your spinach isn't already prepped, you'll need to wash and trim it this way: Pull or cut off the stems, then immerse the leaves in cold water. Dry in a salad spinner or blot with paper towels, and you're ready to go!

Nutty Green Beans

Serving Size: 3/4 cup, Total Servings: 8

3 tablespoons olive oil

1/3 cup chopped walnuts

2 garlic cloves, minced

3 packages (9 ounces each)
   frozen Italian green beans,
   thawed

1/2 cup sun-dried tomatoes,
   reconstituted and slivered

1/2 teaspoon salt

1 In a medium skillet, heat the olive oil over medium-high heat. Sauté the walnuts and garlic for 1 minute.

2 Add the green beans, sun-dried tomatoes, and salt, and sauté for 6 to 7 minutes, or until the green beans are tender. Serve immediately.

Exchanges
2 Vegetable
1-1/2 Fat

Calories............................106
   Calories from Fat............70
Total Fat.............................8 g
   Saturated Fat.....................1 g
Cholesterol.........................0 mg
Sodium............................155 mg
Carbohydrate.....................9 g
   Dietary Fiber.....................3 g
   Sugars...............................4 g
Protein...............................2 g

Good for You!

There are many types of nuts available in your local supermarket, but walnuts are an especially helpful variety, since they're high in omega-3 fatty acids. Those are the "good fats" that have so many health benefits, including regulating blood pressure.

Sweet Onion Sauté

Serving Size: 1 cup, Total Servings: 5

2 tablespoons peanut oil

2 large sweet onions, cut into
　1/2-inch wedges

1 tablespoon sesame seeds

3 medium zucchini, cut in half
　lengthwise then into 1/4-inch
　slices

2 teaspoons light soy sauce

1/8 teaspoon garlic powder

1/8 teaspoon black pepper

1 In a large skillet or wok, heat the oil over medium-high heat. Sauté the onions and sesame seeds over high heat for 5 minutes, stirring frequently.

2 Add the zucchini and cook until the vegetables are just tender.

3 Remove from the heat and stir in the remaining ingredients. Serve immediately.

Exchanges
2 Vegetable
1-1/2 Fat

Calories............................111
　Calories from Fat.............60
Total Fat.............................7 g
　Saturated Fat......................1 g
Cholesterol..........................0 mg
Sodium.............................87 mg
Carbohydrate...................12 g
　Dietary Fiber.....................3 g
　Sugars...............................8 g
Protein..............................3 g

Did You Know...

that there are several varieties of sweet onions? There's the Maui, or Kula, onion, which only grows in the deep-red, volcanic Hawaiian earth; the Georgia Vidalia; the Texas SpringSweet and Texas 1015 SuperSweet varieties; and, last but not least, the Walla Walla variety, grown in Washington State. All of them are exceptionally sweet and flavorful!

Veggie-Lover's Delight

Serving Size: 1 cup, Total Servings: 5

1 package (6 ounces) baby carrots

3 tablespoons butter

3 zucchini, cut into 1-inch chunks

3 yellow squash, cut into 1-inch chunks

1 tablespoon chopped fresh dill weed

1/4 teaspoon onion powder

1/2 teaspoon salt

1/2 teaspoon black pepper

1 Place the carrots in a medium saucepan and add just enough water to cover them. Bring to a boil over medium-high heat and cook for 8 to 10 minutes, or until fork-tender; drain.

2 In a large skillet, over medium heat, melt the butter and add the carrots and remaining ingredients. Stir until well combined. Cook for 6 to 8 minutes, or until the vegetables are tender.

Exchanges
2 Vegetable
1-1/2 Fat

Calories............................116
   Calories from Fat............66
Total Fat..............................7 g
   Saturated Fat......................4 g
Cholesterol......................18 mg
Sodium..........................320 mg
Carbohydrate..................12 g
   Dietary Fiber....................5 g
   Sugars..............................6 g
Protein...............................3 g

Finishing Touch
To give this extra flair, add a sprig of dill weed just before serving. It's a great way to welcome summer!

Oktoberfest Cabbage

Serving Size: 1/2 cup, Total Servings: 12

1 head red cabbage, shredded

2 apples, cored and chopped

1 onion, chopped

1/2 cup cider vinegar

1/4 cup packed light brown sugar

1/4 teaspoon ground cloves

1/2 teaspoon salt

1 In a soup pot, combine all the ingredients and bring to a boil over medium-high heat.

2 Reduce the heat to low, cover, and simmer for 40 to 50 minutes, or until the cabbage is tender.

"Here's the perfect dish to help celebrate Oktoberfest. Crispy autumn apples and red cabbage blend with a homemade sweet-and-sour sauce to make this the perfect go-along for almost any hearty harvest-time main course."

Exchanges

1 Vegetable
1/2 Fruit

Calories 48
   Calories from Fat 3
Total Fat ....0 g
   Saturated Fat ....0 g
Cholesterol ....0 mg
Sodium ....102 mg
Carbohydrate ....12 g
   Dietary Fiber ....2 g
   Sugars ....9 g
Protein ....1 g

Apple Cider Slaw

Serving Size: 1 cup, Total Servings: 16

1/2 of a medium head green cabbage, shredded

1/2 of a medium head red cabbage, shredded

2 large cucumbers, seeded and diced

1 medium onion, finely chopped

1 can (15-1/4 ounces) whole-kernel corn, drained

1/2 cup olive oil

1/2 cup apple cider vinegar

1/3 cup sugar

1-1/2 teaspoons salt

1 In a large bowl, toss together the green and red cabbage, the cucumbers, onion, and corn.

2 In a small bowl, combine the remaining ingredients; pour over the cabbage mixture and toss well. Serve, or cover and chill until ready to serve.

Exchanges
1/2 Carbohydrate
1 Vegetable
1 Fat

Calories............................102
   Calories from Fat............58
Total Fat.............................6 g
   Saturated Fat.....................1 g
Cholesterol..........................0 mg
Sodium............................262 mg
Carbohydrate...................11 g
   Dietary Fiber.....................2 g
   Sugars...............................7 g
Protein...............................1 g

Change of Pace

Don't limit yourself! Go through your veggie bin and you just may find other items to add to this salad. It's sure to add fireworks to your next barbecue.

See Photo Insert

Herbed Asparagus

Serving Size: 1/8 recipe, Total Servings: 8

2 pounds fresh asparagus, trimmed

1 cup reduced-fat Italian dressing

1/2 of a small red bell pepper, diced

2 tablespoons chopped fresh parsley

1/2 teaspoon dried chives

1 hard-boiled egg, finely chopped (optional)

1 Fill a soup pot with 1 inch of water and bring to a boil over high heat. Add the asparagus, cover, and steam for 4 to 6 minutes, or until fork-tender. Remove the asparagus and plunge it into a large bowl of ice water to stop the cooking process.

2 In a 9" × 13" baking dish, combine the Italian dressing, red pepper, parsley, and chives; mix well.

3 Remove the asparagus from the water, drain well, and add to the baking dish, coating it completely with the dressing mixture.

4 Cover and chill for at least 2 hours before serving. Just before serving, sprinkle with the chopped egg, if desired.

Exchanges
1 Vegetable

Calories	31
Calories from Fat	11
Total Fat	1 g
Saturated Fat	0 g
Cholesterol	0 mg
Sodium	456 mg
Carbohydrate	5 g
Dietary Fiber	1 g
Sugars	2 g
Protein	1 g

Did You Know...

that the best way to trim fresh asparagus is by holding each spear and breaking off the stem end at the exact point where the tender part meets the tough part? It's something you can actually feel, so go ahead and get snapping!

See Photo Insert

Desserts

Chocolate Cheese Pie

Serving Size: 1 slice, Total Servings: 10

2 eggs

3/4 cup sugar

1 package (8 ounces) reduced-fat
   cream cheese, softened

3/4 cup half-and-half

2 tablespoons all-purpose flour

1/4 teaspoon baking soda

1/8 teaspoon salt

2 squares (1 ounce each)
   unsweetened chocolate,
   melted

1 teaspoon vanilla extract

One frozen 9-inch deep-dish pie
   shell, thawed

1 Preheat the oven to 325°F.

2 In a small bowl, beat the eggs and sugar. In a large bowl, beat the cream cheese until creamy. Add the half-and-half, flour, baking soda, and salt; mix well. Add the egg mixture, the melted chocolate, and the vanilla; beat well, then pour into the unbaked pie shell.

3 Bake for 50 to 55 minutes, or until a wooden toothpick inserted in the center comes out clean.

4 Allow to cool, then cover and chill for at least 2 hours before serving.

Exchanges
2 Carbohydrate
3 Fat

Calories............................259
   Calories from Fat..........141
Total Fat...........................16 g
   Saturated Fat.....................8 g
Cholesterol.......................65 mg
Sodium............................268 mg
Carbohydrate...................26 g
   Dietary Fiber.....................1 g
   Sugars.............................16 g
Protein..............................6 g

Good for You!

Whether you're watching your weight, monitoring your diabetes, or both, this dessert is rich and satisfying … and it won't make you feel guilty.

Polka Dot Peach Pie

Serving Size: 1 slice, Total Servings: 8

5 medium ripe peaches, peeled and sliced OR 1 package (16 ounces) frozen peaches, thawed

1/3 cup sugar

1/4 cup all-purpose flour

3 tablespoons butter, melted

1 teaspoon vanilla extract

1 refrigerated pie crust (1/2 of a 15-ounce package)

1 Preheat the oven to 375°F.

2 In a large bowl, combine all the ingredients except the pie crust; mix well, and spoon into a 9-inch pie plate.

3 Place the pie crust on a work surface and, using a 1-inch round cookie cutter or the top from a plastic water bottle, form polka dots by cutting out seven circles from the center, leaving a 1-inch border around the edge.

4 Place the crust over the peach mixture. Pinch the crust to the pie plate and trim the edges to seal, then flute, if desired.

5 Bake for 35 to 40 minutes, or until the crust is golden and the filling is bubbly. Let cool before serving.

Exchanges
2 Carbohydrate
2 Fat

Calories	203
Calories from Fat	91
Total Fat	10 g
Saturated Fat	5 g
Cholesterol	15 mg
Sodium	126 mg
Carbohydrate	27 g
Dietary Fiber	1 g
Sugars	12 g
Protein	1 g

Did You Know...

that fresh peaches are low in calories, they contain no fat or sodium, and are a good source of vitamin A? When choosing peaches, check for fresh peach fragrance and select ones that are firm to slightly soft, and free from bruises.

Flashy Fruit Tarts

Serving Size: 1 tart, Total Servings: 6

1 package (8 ounces) reduced-fat cream cheese, softened

2 tablespoons orange marmalade

1/4 cup sugar

6 single-serving graham cracker tart shells

2 kiwifruit, peeled, halved, and sliced

1/2 cup fresh raspberries

1. In a medium bowl, with an electric beater on medium speed, beat the cream cheese, marmalade, and sugar for 2 minutes, or until well combined.

2. Spoon the mixture evenly into the tart shells, then top with the kiwi slices and raspberries.

3. Cover loosely and chill for at least 2 hours before serving.

Exchanges
2-1/2 Carbohydrate
2-1/2 Fat

Calories............................283
   Calories from Fat..........122
Total Fat............................14 g
   Saturated Fat......................6 g
Cholesterol........................27 mg
Sodium............................311 mg
Carbohydrate....................34 g
   Dietary Fiber.....................2 g
   Sugars................................23 g
Protein................................5 g

Finishing Touch
We can decorate this to match any holiday—strawberries and raspberries for Valentine's Day; all kiwi, or kiwi and mint, for St. Patrick's Day; strawberries and blueberries for Memorial Day and the Fourth of July ... you get it!

Banana Peanut Butter Cake

Serving Size: 1 wedge, Total Servings: 8

3/4 cup all-purpose flour

1/2 teaspoon baking powder

1/2 teaspoon baking soda

1/4 teaspoon salt

1/4 cup (1/2 stick) unsalted butter, softened

1/3 cup sugar

1 egg

1/4 cup reduced-fat peanut butter

2 tablespoons reduced-fat sour cream

1 large ripe banana, mashed

1 Preheat the oven to 350°F. Coat an 8-inch round cake pan with non-stick cooking spray.

2 In a small bowl, combine the flour, baking powder, baking soda, and salt; mix well and set aside.

3 In a large bowl, cream the butter and sugar. Add the egg, peanut butter, sour cream, and banana; mix well. Add the flour mixture; mix well, then spread into the cake pan.

4 Bake for 25 to 30 minutes, or until a wooden toothpick inserted in the center comes out clean. Let cool in the pan for 10 minutes, then remove from the pan to cool completely before cutting into wedges.

Exchanges
1-1/2 Carbohydrate
2 Fat

Calories	198
Calories from Fat	86
Total Fat	10 g
Saturated Fat	5 g
Cholesterol	43 mg
Sodium	231 mg
Carbohydrate	25 g
Dietary Fiber	1 g
Sugars	12 g
Protein	4 g

"Why not make this to commemorate Elvis Presley's birthday on January 8? 'The King' would love this devilish delight that teams his eternal favorites: peanut butter and bananas. Remember, even though peanut butter is a good source of protein, it's high in fat, and should be eaten in moderation ... so save this one for special occasions."

Chocolate Cheesecake

Serving Size: 1 slice, Total Servings: 16

1-1/2 cups graham cracker crumbs

1/3 cup butter, melted

3 packages (8 ounces each) reduced-fat cream cheese, softened

1 cup plus 2 tablespoons sugar, divided

4 eggs

2 teaspoons vanilla extract, divided

1/4 cup unsweetened cocoa

1 container (16 ounces) reduced-fat sour cream

1. Preheat the oven to 350°F.

2. In a medium bowl, combine the graham cracker crumbs and butter; mix well. Press into a 10-inch springform pan, covering the bottom and sides. Chill while preparing the filling.

3. In a large bowl, blend the cream cheese and 1 cup sugar with an electric beater. Add the eggs one at a time, beating well after each addition. Add 1 teaspoon vanilla and the cocoa; mix well, then pour into the chilled crust.

4. Bake for 50 to 55 minutes, or until firm. Remove from the oven and let cool for 5 minutes. (Leave the oven on.)

5. In a medium bowl, with a spoon, mix the sour cream and the remaining 2 tablespoons sugar and 1 teaspoon vanilla until well combined. Spread over the top of the cheesecake and bake for 5 minutes.

6. Let cool, then refrigerate overnight before serving.

Exchanges
1-1/2 Carbohydrate
1 Medium-Fat Meat
2-1/2 Fat

Calories............................279
   Calories from Fat..........156
Total Fat...........................17 g
   Saturated Fat...................11 g
Cholesterol.....................102 mg
Sodium...........................300 mg
Carbohydrate...................24 g
   Dietary Fiber.....................1 g
   Sugars...............................18 g
Protein..............................9 g

Finishing Touch
What could make this already decadent-looking and -tasting treat any more decadent, while staying within the guidelines of our healthy meal plan? Garnish it with a few fresh strawberries or raspberries. Wow! Wow!

Photo on book cover

Buttery Squash Roll

Serving Size: 1 slice, Total Servings: 10

3/4 cup all-purpose flour

1 teaspoon baking powder

2 teaspoons ground cinnamon

1 teaspoon ground ginger

1/2 teaspoon ground nutmeg

1/2 teaspoon salt

3 eggs

3/4 cup granulated sugar

1 package (11 ounces) frozen butternut squash, thawed and drained

1-1/2 teaspoons vanilla extract, divided

1/2 cup confectioners' sugar, plus extra for sprinkling

1 package (8 ounces) reduced-fat cream cheese, softened

1/4 cup (1/2 stick) butter, softened

1. Preheat the oven to 375°F. Coat a 10" × 15" rimmed baking sheet with non-stick cooking spray.

2. In a medium bowl, combine the flour, baking powder, cinnamon, ginger, nutmeg, and salt; mix well and set aside.

3. In a large bowl, with an electric beater on high speed, beat the eggs for 4 to 5 minutes, until fluffy. Beat in the granulated sugar, squash, and 1 teaspoon vanilla. Fold in the flour mixture until well blended, then pour the batter onto the baking sheet.

4. Bake for 12 to 15 minutes, or until a wooden toothpick inserted in the center comes out clean. Invert the cake onto a clean kitchen towel that has been sprinkled with confectioners' sugar. While still hot, roll up the cake in the towel jelly-roll style from a narrow end; cool on a wire rack. When cool, unroll the cake and remove the towel.

5. In a small bowl, with an electric beater on medium speed, beat the 1/2 cup confectioners' sugar, the cream cheese, butter, and the remaining 1/2 teaspoon vanilla until creamy. Spread over the cake, then roll up again. Cover loosely and chill for at least 2 hours.

6. When ready to serve, sprinkle the roll with confectioners' sugar, then slice.

Exchanges

2 Carbohydrate
2 Fat

Calories	249
Calories from Fat	99
Total Fat	11 g
Saturated Fat	7 g
Cholesterol	92 mg
Sodium	315 mg
Carbohydrate	32 g
Dietary Fiber	1 g
Sugars	22 g
Protein	6 g

Good for You!

This Thanksgiving, instead of pie, try this on for size! It's chock-full of vitamins A and C, which are helpful in preventing cancer and heart disease. Now that's something to be thankful for!

Cinnamon Banana Cake

Serving Size: 1 square, Total Servings: 16

1-1/2 cups all-purpose flour

1/2 cup sugar

2 teaspoons baking powder

1 teaspoon baking soda

2 teaspoons ground cinnamon

1/2 teaspoon salt

1 cup low-fat vanilla yogurt

2 ripe bananas, mashed

2 tablespoons vegetable oil

1 egg

1 teaspoon vanilla extract

1 Preheat the oven to 400°F. Coat an 8-inch square baking dish with non-stick cooking spray.

2 In a large bowl, combine the flour, sugar, baking powder, baking soda, cinnamon, and salt; mix well. Add the yogurt, bananas, oil, egg, and vanilla; mix until well blended, then spread into the baking dish.

3 Bake for 22 to 25 minutes, or until golden and a wooden toothpick inserted in the center comes out clean.

4 Let cool, then cut into squares.

Exchanges
1-1/2 Carbohydrate
1/2 Fat

Calories 116
   Calories from Fat 22
Total Fat .... 2 g
   Saturated Fat .... 0 g
Cholesterol .... 15 mg
Sodium .... 210 mg
Carbohydrate .... 21 g
   Dietary Fiber .... 1 g
   Sugars .... 11 g
Protein .... 2 g

Finishing Touch

Lightly dust with confectioners' sugar before serving, and, for extra flair, garnish with thin fresh banana slices.

Peppermint Cheesecake

Serving Size: 1 slice, Total Servings: 10

2 packages (8 ounces each) 1/3-less-fat cream cheese, softened

1/2 cup sugar

2 eggs

3/4 cup low-fat sour cream

1 teaspoon vanilla extract

1 teaspoon peppermint extract

6 drops red food color

One 9-inch reduced-fat graham cracker pie crust

Whipped cream and mini candy canes for garnish (optional)

1 Preheat the oven to 350°F. In a large bowl, beat the cream cheese and sugar until light and fluffy. Add the eggs and beat well. Add the sour cream and vanilla; mix well.

2 Place 1/2 cup of the mixture in a small bowl and stir in the peppermint extract and food color; mix well. Pour the remaining cream cheese mixture into the pie crust; smooth the top.

3 Drop the peppermint mixture by spoonfuls into the mixture in the crust and swirl with a knife to create a marbled effect.

4 Bake for 30 to 35 minutes, or until the edges are set. (The center will be slightly loose.) Allow to cool for 1 hour, then cover and chill for at least 6 hours before serving.

5 Top each slice with a dollop of whipped cream and a mini candy cane, if desired.

Exchanges
1-1/2 Carbohydrate
1 Medium-Fat Meat
2 Fat

Calories............................265
   Calories from Fat..........130
Total Fat..........................14 g
   Saturated Fat.....................8 g
Cholesterol.......................80 mg
Sodium.............................292 mg
Carbohydrate...................25 g
   Dietary Fiber.....................0 g
   Sugars.............................17 g
Protein.............................8 g

Change of Pace
You'll be feeling "in the pink" with this one, 'cause this colorful dessert is a refreshing change from traditional cheesecake.

Peanut Butter Cookies

Serving Size: 2 cookies, Total Servings: 18

2/3 cup all-purpose flour

1/2 teaspoon baking soda

1/2 teaspoon baking powder

1/4 teaspoon salt

1/3 cup vegetable shortening

1/3 cup reduced-fat peanut butter

2 tablespoons light brown sugar

2 tablespoons granulated sugar

2 eggs, well beaten

1 Preheat the oven to 375°F. Coat baking sheets with nonstick cooking spray.

2 In a medium bowl, combine the flour, baking soda, baking powder, and salt; mix well.

3 In a large bowl, combine the shortening and peanut butter until creamy, then gradually add the brown and granulated sugars until blended. Add the beaten eggs and mix thoroughly.

4 Add the flour mixture to the peanut butter mixture and mix until a soft dough forms. Drop by 1/2-teaspoonfuls onto the baking sheets. Bake for 8 to 10 minutes, or until golden.

Exchanges
1/2 Carbohydrate
1 Fat

Calories............................100
    Calories from Fat............58
Total Fat.............................6 g
    Saturated Fat.....................1 g
Cholesterol........................24 mg
Sodium............................112 mg
Carbohydrate.....................9 g
    Dietary Fiber.....................0 g
    Sugars................................4 g
Protein...............................2 g

"You don't have to be a kid to love peanut butter—or cookies, for that matter! This recipe combines the two favorites into one ageless treat."

Minty Leprechaun Cookies

Serving Size: 2 cookies, Total Servings: 12

2 egg whites (at room temperature)

2 drops green food color

1/2 teaspoon vanilla extract

1/8 teaspoon mint extract

1/3 cup sugar

1/3 cup mini semisweet chocolate chips

1 Preheat the oven to 325°F. Coat nonstick baking sheets with non-stick cooking spray.

2 In a large bowl, beat the egg whites, food color, and vanilla and mint extracts with an electric mixer until soft peaks form. Gradually beat in the sugar; beat until stiff peaks form.

3 Fold in the chocolate chips, then drop by tablespoonfuls onto the baking sheets.

4 Bake for 10 minutes. Turn off the oven but leave the cookies in the oven until cool.

Exchanges
1/2 Carbohydrate

Calories	47
Calories from Fat	13
Total Fat	1 g
Saturated Fat	1 g
Cholesterol	0 mg
Sodium	10 mg
Carbohydrate	8 g
Dietary Fiber	0 g
Sugars	8 g
Protein	1 g

"Turn your kids into lucky leprechauns and let them share these magical disappearing treats with their friends on St. Patrick's Day. And make sure to bake an extra batch to take to the office so your co-workers won't be 'green with envy!' "

Gingerbread Cookies

Serving Size: 2 cookies, Total Servings: 30

1 cup (2 sticks) butter, softened

1/4 cup sugar

1/2 cup molasses

1 egg

3-1/2 cups all-purpose flour

1/2 teaspoon baking soda

1-1/2 teaspoons ground ginger

1 teaspoon ground cinnamon

1 In a medium bowl, cream together the butter, sugar, molasses, and egg.

2 In another medium bowl, combine the flour, baking soda, ginger, and cinnamon. Gradually add to the butter mixture; mix until smooth.

3 Refrigerate dough for 2 hours or overnight.

4 Preheat the oven to 375°F. Coat baking sheets with nonstick cooking spray.

5 Roll out the dough onto a lightly floured surface to 1/8-inch thickness. Cut into your favorite shapes with cookie cutters and place on the baking sheets.

6 Bake for 7 to 8 minutes, or until golden around the edges. Remove to a wire rack to cool completely.

Exchanges
1 Carbohydrate
1 Fat

Calories	131
Calories from Fat	58
Total Fat	6 g
Saturated Fat	4 g
Cholesterol	23 mg
Sodium	88 mg
Carbohydrate	17 g
Dietary Fiber	0 g
Sugars	5 g
Protein	2 g

Good for You!

In addition to gingerbread houses and ginger-flavored cookies being Christmastime favorites, ginger itself is an all-around "good guy." Studies have found that ginger provides a load of health benefits, including soothing unsettled tummies, reducing blood cholesterol, and a whole lot more!

Creamy Tortoni

Serving Size: 1 tortoni, Total Servings: 12

1 quart no-sugar-added light vanilla ice cream

1-1/2 cups frozen light whipped topping, thawed

1-1/2 teaspoons almond extract

1/4 cup plus 2 tablespoons chopped blanched almonds, divided

6 maraschino cherries, halved

1. Line 12 muffin cups with paper baking cups.

2. In a large bowl, soften the ice cream (see below). Fold in the whipped topping and mix well. Add the almond extract and 1/4 cup almonds; mix well.

3. Place about 1/3 cup of the mixture into each muffin cup. Sprinkle evenly with the remaining 2 tablespoons almonds.

4. Cover the muffin cups and place in the freezer for 2 to 3 hours. Just before serving, garnish each with a maraschino cherry half.

Exchanges
1 Carbohydrate
1 Fat

Calories............................106
  Calories from Fat............50
Total Fat..............................6 g
  Saturated Fat......................3 g
Cholesterol........................17 mg
Sodium..............................36 mg
Carbohydrate....................11 g
  Dietary Fiber......................1 g
  Sugars................................6 g
Protein..............................3 g

Preparation Tip

To soften the ice cream, break it up in a mixing bowl and stir with a wooden spoon. Do not let the ice cream reach the melting point.

Not-Fried "Fried" Ice Cream

Serving Size: 1 scoop, Total Servings: 8

1 quart no-sugar-added light vanilla ice cream

2-1/2 cups oven-toasted corn cereal, coarsely crushed

1 tablespoon butter, melted

1 tablespoon sugar

1 teaspoon ground cinnamon

1 Line a large rimmed baking sheet with wax paper.

2 With a large spoon or an ice cream scoop, form the ice cream into 8 solid balls, each about 2-1/2 inches in diameter. Place on the baking sheet, then place in the freezer for about 1 hour.

3 Meanwhile, preheat the oven to 350°F. Coat another large rimmed baking sheet with nonstick cooking spray. In a medium bowl, combine the remaining ingredients; mix well and spread on the baking sheet.

4 Bake for 5 to 7 minutes, or until crisp and lightly browned. Remove to a shallow dish and allow to cool completely.

5 Replace the wax paper on the first baking sheet. Roll the frozen ice cream balls in the cereal mixture, coating on all sides, then place on the baking sheet and freeze for 2 to 3 hours, or until the ice cream is firm; serve immediately, or cover and keep frozen until ready to serve.

Exchanges
1-1/2 Carbohydrate
1 Fat

Calories............................159
   Calories from Fat............54
Total Fat..............................6 g
   Saturated Fat......................3 g
Cholesterol........................29 mg
Sodium..............................204 mg
Carbohydrate....................24 g
   Dietary Fiber......................1 g
   Sugars................................8 g
Protein.................................4 g

Good for You!

I've made this recipe for years, but now I've made a few adjustments and reduced the calories and fat—and it's just as satisfying ... and better for us!

Cookies 'n' Cream Sandwiches

Serving Size: 1 sandwich, Total Servings: 24

1 package (16 ounces) reduced-fat cream-filled chocolate sandwich cookies, crushed (see Preparation Tip)

1/4 cup (1/2 stick) butter, melted

1/2 gallon no-sugar-added light vanilla ice cream, slightly softened

1 Place the crushed cookies in a medium bowl. Add the melted butter; mix well, then press half of the mixture firmly into the bottom of an aluminum foil-lined 9" × 13" baking pan.

2 Spread the softened ice cream over the cookie mixture, then gently press the remaining cookie mixture over the ice cream.

3 Cover and freeze for at least 6 hours. Cut into squares and serve, or wrap each square individually and keep frozen for an always-ready snack.

Exchanges
1-1/2 Carbohydrate
1 Fat

Calories	159
Calories from Fat	63
Total Fat	7 g
Saturated Fat	3 g
Cholesterol	22 mg
Sodium	161 mg
Carbohydrate	22 g
Dietary Fiber	1 g
Sugars	12 g
Protein	3 g

Preparation Tip

You can crush the sandwich cookies in a food processor or by sealing them in a resealable plastic storage bag and using a rolling pin.

Frozen Cheesecake Pie

Serving Size: 1 slice, Total Servings: 12

1 package (8 ounces) reduced-fat cream cheese, softened

1/2 cup sugar

1 cup reduced-fat sour cream

2 teaspoons vanilla extract

1 container (8 ounces) frozen light whipped topping, thawed

One 9-inch reduced-fat graham cracker pie crust

1 In a large bowl, beat the cream cheese until smooth; gradually beat in the sugar.

2 Blend in the sour cream and vanilla. Fold in the whipped topping until well combined, then spoon the mixture into the crust.

3 Freeze until firm, then slice and serve frozen.

Exchanges
1-1/2 Carbohydrate
2 Fat

Calories............................215
   Calories from Fat............90
Total Fat............................10 g
   Saturated Fat......................7 g
Cholesterol........................20 mg
Sodium............................161 mg
Carbohydrate....................25 g
   Dietary Fiber......................0 g
   Sugars..............................16 g
Protein ....4 g

Finishing Touch

What a super refresher for a summer holiday bash! And on Memorial Day or the Fourth of July, you might want to add a splash of red, white, and blue with a bit of fresh fruit, or blueberry or cherry pie filling, topped with a dollop of billowy white whipped topping!

Chocoholic's Sherbet

Serving Size: 1/2 cup, Total Servings: 8

3/4 cup sugar

1/2 cup unsweetened cocoa

1/2 cup hot water

2 cups low-fat (1%) milk

1/4 cup cold water

1 In a small saucepan, combine the sugar and cocoa over low heat. Slowly stir in the hot water and continue stirring for 2 to 3 minutes, or until the sugar is dissolved.

2 Remove the mixture from the heat and gradually stir in the milk. Pour into a 9" × 13" glass baking dish, cover, and freeze for 4 to 6 hours, or until hardened.

3 Break up the frozen mixture and place in a blender or food processor fitted with its metal cutting blade; add the cold water.

4 Blend or process until smooth and light-colored. Pour into an airtight freezer-safe container; seal and freeze for at least 2 hours, or until set.

Exchanges
1-1/2 Carbohydrate

Calories	107
Calories from Fat	13
Total Fat	1 g
Saturated Fat	0 g
Cholesterol	2 mg
Sodium	31 mg
Carbohydrate	24 g
Dietary Fiber	2 g
Sugars	21 g
Protein	3 g

"All three of my children married chocoholics, so you can guess who I make this for! If you're like them, and you can never get enough chocolate, then this one's for you, too. It's got all the rich chocolate taste you could want … without any of the guilt."

Fruit Stand Surprise

Serving Size: 1/2 cup fruit plus cantaloupe wedge, Total Servings: 10

1 container (8 ounces) low-fat
   vanilla yogurt

2 teaspoons light brown sugar

1 quart fresh strawberries,
   washed, hulled, and sliced

2 bananas, peeled and sliced

2 kiwis, peeled and sliced

1 cantaloupe, peeled, seeded, and
   cut into 10 wedges

2 tablespoons sliced almonds

1 In a large bowl, combine the yogurt
   and brown sugar; mix well. Add the
   strawberries, bananas, and kiwi;
   toss until the fruit is well coated.

2 Place each cantaloupe wedge on a
   serving plate. Spoon equal amounts
   of the fruit mixture over them and
   top with the sliced almonds. Serve
   immediately.

Exchanges
1-1/2 Fruit
1/2 Fat

Calories 110
   Calories from Fat 15
Total Fat ....2 g
   Saturated Fat ....0 g
Cholesterol ....2 mg
Sodium ....21 mg
Carbohydrate ....23 g
   Dietary Fiber ....4 g
   Sugars ....18 g
Protein ....3 g

Good for You!

Summer is the easiest time of
the year to get those all-impor-
tant five-a-day servings of fruit
and vegetables. With all our seasonal favorites picked fresh and
available in our markets, a
refreshing fruit-laden dish
like this makes any day
seem like cause for
celebration!

The Great Grape Crumble

Serving Size: 1/12 recipe, Total Servings: 12

6 cups seedless green or red grapes

1/4 cup plus 2 tablespoons sugar, divided

1/2 cup (1 stick) butter, melted and divided

1 cup plus 2 tablespoons all-purpose flour, divided

1 teaspoon orange zest

1/8 teaspoon ground nutmeg

1/2 cup reduced-fat sour cream

1 egg, beaten

1 teaspoon baking powder

1 Preheat the oven to 375°F. Coat a 9" × 13" baking dish with nonstick cooking spray.

2 In a large bowl, combine the grapes, 1/4 cup sugar, 1/4 cup melted butter, 2 tablespoons flour, the orange zest, and nutmeg; mix well and pour into the baking dish.

3 In a medium bowl, combine the remaining 2 tablespoons sugar, 1/4 cup melted butter, 1 cup flour, the sour cream, egg, and baking powder; mix well and spoon evenly over the grape mixture.

4 Bake for 45 minutes, or until the crust is golden and the juices are thickened. Allow to cool slightly, then serve warm.

Exchanges
2 Carbohydrate
2 Fat

Calories............................210
  Calories from Fat.............85
Total Fat.............................9 g
  Saturated Fat.....................5 g
Cholesterol........................41 mg
Sodium...............................123 mg
Carbohydrate...................30 g
  Dietary Fiber.....................1 g
  Sugars...............................18 g
Protein...............................3 g

"I came across this dish recently while in Australia, where I was serving as a diabetes ambassador. It's really satisfying, since the natural sweetness of the grapes helps calm those sweet cravings. I'm sure you get those from time to time, 'cause I sure do!"

"Berry-licious" Parfait

Serving Size: 1 parfait, Total Servings: 4

1 pint strawberries, washed, hulled, and sliced

3 tablespoons strawberry all-fruit spread, melted

1 package (3 ounces) reduced-fat cream cheese, softened

1 tablespoon fat-free (skim) milk

1 tablespoon lemon juice

1 tablespoon sugar

1/2 cup frozen light whipped topping, thawed

1/4 cup graham cracker crumbs

1 In a medium bowl, toss the strawberries and fruit spread; set aside.

2 In another medium bowl, beat the cream cheese, milk, lemon juice, and sugar until smooth; fold in the whipped topping.

3 Equally divide half of the strawberry mixture among four parfait glasses, then sprinkle with half of the graham cracker crumbs, and top with half of the cream cheese mixture. Repeat the layers, and serve immediately, or cover and chill until ready to serve.

Exchanges
1-1/2 Carbohydrate
1 Fat

Calories	165
Calories from Fat	57
Total Fat	6 g
Saturated Fat	4 g
Cholesterol	15 mg
Sodium	131 mg
Carbohydrate	24 g
Dietary Fiber	2 g
Sugars	16 g
Protein	3 g

"How could anything this creamy, this decadent, this fresh-tasting be guilt-free? Well, it is, 'cause the low-fat ingredients allow us to indulge once in a while."

Creamy Pumpkin Mousse

Serving Size: 1/2 cup, Total Servings: 10

1 can (16 ounces) solid-pack pure pumpkin

1 package (6-serving size) instant sugar-free vanilla pudding mix

1/4 cup low-fat (1%) milk

1 teaspoon ground cinnamon

2 cups frozen light whipped topping, thawed

1 In a medium bowl, with an electric beater on medium speed, beat the pumpkin, pudding mix, milk, and cinnamon until well blended.

2 Fold in the whipped topping until thoroughly blended, then spoon into a serving bowl. Cover loosely and chill until ready to serve.

"This is a perfect dessert to make with the kids around Halloween. It's super-easy, and super-quick! Believe me, as word spreads, their friends will be knocking at your door … but not for candy, so be sure to have plenty on hand!"

See Photo Insert

Exchanges
1 Carbohydrate

Calories	65
Calories from Fat	16
Total Fat	2 g
Saturated Fat	2 g
Cholesterol	0 mg
Sodium	207 mg
Carbohydrate	11 g
Dietary Fiber	1 g
Sugars	3 g
Protein	1 g

Homemade Chocolate Pudding

Serving Size: 1/2 cup, Total Servings: 4

1/2 cup sugar

3 tablespoons cornstarch

2 tablespoons unsweetened cocoa

1/4 teaspoon salt

2-1/4 cups low-fat (1%) milk

1 teaspoon vanilla extract

1 In a medium saucepan, combine the sugar, cornstarch, cocoa, and salt. Gradually stir in the milk and bring to a boil over medium heat, stirring constantly.

2 Remove from the heat and stir in the vanilla. Allow to cool slightly, then transfer to serving dishes, cover, and chill for 2 hours, or until set.

Exchanges

2-1/2 Carbohydrate

Calories	181
Calories from Fat	17
Total Fat	2 g
Saturated Fat	1 g
Cholesterol	6 mg
Sodium	215 mg
Carbohydrate	38 g
Dietary Fiber	1 g
Sugars	30 g
Protein	5 g

Preparation Tip

Nothing welcomes the kids home from school more than a homemade favorite like chocolate pudding. If you want to prevent a skin from forming on the top of the pudding, simply place sheets of wax paper directly on the surface of the pudding. Either way, everybody is sure to enjoy the thick texture and rich chocolate flavor of this cherished childhood treat.

Almond Fudge Brownies

Serving Size: 1 square, Total Servings: 16

2 tablespoons butter, softened

1 cup sugar

1/2 cup unsweetened applesauce

1 egg

2 teaspoons vanilla extract

1/2 cup unsweetened cocoa
  powder

3/4 cup all-purpose flour

1/4 cup sliced almonds

1 Preheat the oven to 350°F. Coat an 8-inch square baking dish with nonstick cooking spray.

2 In a medium bowl, using an electric beater on medium speed, beat the butter, sugar, applesauce, egg, and vanilla. Slowly beat in the cocoa and flour. Pour the batter into the baking dish and top with the almonds.

3 Bake for 25 to 30 minutes, or until a wooden toothpick inserted in the center comes out clean. Cool completely before cutting.

Exchanges
1-1/2 Carbohydrate
1/2 Fat

Calories	108
Calories from Fat	29
Total Fat	3 g
Saturated Fat	1 g
Cholesterol	17 mg
Sodium	19 mg
Carbohydrate	19 g
Dietary Fiber	1 g
Sugars	13 g
Protein	2 g

Good for You!

Almonds are an amazing nutritional powerhouse since they're chock-full of vitamins, minerals, and "good fats"—the monounsaturated fats, which are associated with decreased risk of heart disease.

See Photo
Insert

Baked Rice Pudding

Serving Size: 1/2 cup, Total Servings: 9

4 cups low-fat (1%) milk

1 cup whole- or long-grain rice, uncooked

1/4 cup sugar

2 tablespoons butter, melted

1/2 teaspoon ground cinnamon

1/4 teaspoon ground nutmeg

1/4 teaspoon salt

1 Preheat the oven to 325°F. Coat an 8-inch square baking dish with non-stick cooking spray.

2 In a medium bowl, combine all the ingredients; mix well, then pour into the baking dish.

3 Bake for 1-1/2 hours, or until a knife inserted in the center comes out clean.

4 Let cool, then cover and chill for at least 2 hours before serving.

Exchanges
2 Carbohydrate
1/2 Fat

Calories............................164
   Calories from Fat.............35
Total Fat.............................4 g
   Saturated Fat......................3 g
Cholesterol.......................11 mg
Sodium............................146 mg
Carbohydrate...................27 g
   Dietary Fiber.....................0 g
   Sugars...............................10 g
Protein...............................5 g

"Boy, does this bring me back to my childhood, when Mom was always baking up comforting treats for our family—especially when the leaves started changing colors every autumn. It's just right for a cool fall evening."

Recipe Index

About the American Diabetes Association

The American Diabetes Association is the nation's leading voluntary health organization supporting diabetes research, information, and advocacy. Its mission is to prevent and cure diabetes and to improve the lives of all people affected by diabetes. The American Diabetes Association is the leading publisher of comprehensive diabetes information. Its huge library of practical and authoritative books for people with diabetes covers every aspect of self-care—cooking and nutrition, fitness, weight control, medications, complications, emotional issues, and general self-care.

To order American Diabetes Association books: Call 1-800-232-6733. http://store.diabetes.org [Note: there is no need to use **www** when typing this particular Web address]

To join the American Diabetes Association: Call 1-800-806-7801. www.diabetes.org/membership

For more information about diabetes or ADA programs and services: Call 1-800-342-2383. E-mail: Customerservice@diabetes.org www.diabetes.org

To locate an ADA/NCQA Recognized Provider of quality diabetes care in your area: www.ncqa.org/dprp/

To find an ADA Recognized Education Program in your area: Call 1-888-232-0822. www.diabetes.org/recognition/education.asp

To join the fight to increase funding for diabetes research, end discrimination, and improve insurance coverage: Call 1-800-342-2383. www.diabetes.org/advocacy

To find out how you can get involved with the programs in your community: Call 1-800-342-2383. See below for program Web addresses.

- *American Diabetes Month:* Educational activities aimed at those diagnosed with diabetes—month of November. www.diabetes.org/ADM
- *American Diabetes Alert:* Annual public awareness campaign to find the undiagnosed—held the fourth Tuesday in March. www.diabetes.org/alert
- *The Diabetes Assistance & Resources Program (DAR):* diabetes awareness program targeted to the Latino community. www.diabetes.org/DAR
- *African American Program:* diabetes awareness program targeted to the African American community. www.diabetes.org/africanamerican
- *Awakening the Spirit: Pathways to Diabetes Prevention & Control:* diabetes awareness program targeted to the Native American community. www.diabetes.org/awakening

To find out about an important research project regarding type 2 diabetes: www.diabetes.org/ada/research.asp

To obtain information on making a planned gift or charitable bequest: Call 1-888-700-7029. www.diabetes.org/ada/plan.asp

To make a donation or memorial contribution: Call 1-800-342-2383. www.diabetes.org/ada/cont.asp